# Thereafter Johnnie

## *Carolivia Herron*

1stBooks - rev. 2/14/01

# ACKNOWLEDGMENTS

Georgia Carol Johnson Herron; Oscar S. Herron; Charles W. Thomas—professor, dean, colonel, captain; Johnnie Thomas; *Nethula Journal; River Styx; Callaloo;* Kathy Anderson; Ethelbert Miller; Howard University Moorland-Spingarn Room; U. S. National Park Service; U. S. Bureau of Land Management of New Mexico; the Sangre de Cristo Mountains of Santa Fe, New Mexico; Eastern Baptist College; Villanova University; the University of Pennsylvania Comparative Literature Department; Stuart Curran; Joseph Wittreich; Jean Alter; Saul Morson; Harvard University African American Studies, History, Literature and Comparative Literature Departments; Barbara Keifer Lewalski; Werner Sollors; the late Nathan Huggins; Helen Vendler; Seamus Heaney; Skip Gates; Patsy Yaeger; Svetlana Boym; Padan Aram; Adams House; Dana School; Black Arts Festival; Villanova University English Department; George Murphy; Earl Bader; Paul Gillespie; Mount Holyoke College; Richard Johnson of Mount Holyoke College; Mary McHenry; Bill Quillian; Odyssey Book Store; Lorraine Ramsey; University of Binghamton; Thomas Glave; Anne Higginbottom, Elizabeth Rosenberg; Donnae Jackson; Esther Mae Davin; Allegra Patrice Kelly McManus; Robert L. Simmons; Sally; the Western Herrons: Smitty, Theresa, Joseph, Jeffrey; Jeannie Sanders; Cassandra F. Richard; Marquita Lightfoot; Rosemary Crockett; Cynthia Sollor; Ethan Bumas; Jonathan Bumas; Haile Bagashao Miriam; James Fitzpatrick; D.C. Public Library; Library of Congress; Cummington Community of the Arts; MacDowell Artists Colony; Gloria Naylor; Carlos Fuentes; Third Baptist Church of Washington, D.C.; Bunting Institute of Radcliffe College; Folger Shakespeare Library; Beinecke Library of Yale University; Smithsonian Institute Museum of American Art; Freer Gallery of Art; National Endowment for the Humanities; Rockefeller Foundation; Fulbright Fellowships; Jonathan E. Kolb; Puerto Escondido, México; Holyoke State Forest; Harvard Hillel, Tifereth Israel Congregation of Washington, D.C.; John Milton; Jeremiah.

*Thereafter Johnnie* by Carolivia Herron weaves together beauty, sorrow and unwavering tragic vision attached to the fall of an African American family through incest. The plot is simple, a liaison between a father, John Christopher, and Patricia, one of three daughters, produces their daughter Johnnie. This story becomes intricate through visionary lyricism; through connections with slavery, religion, and the flaws of national destiny; through echoes of African American folk rhythms and the epic poems of Europe and Africa; and most importantly, through thematic correlation with Washington, D.C., Washington City. The novel has seven characters: the parents Camille and John Christopher; the three daughters Cynthia Jane, Patricia, and Eva; the child of incest, Johnnie; and the Mexican woman Diotima who is Patricia's friend and Johnnie's caretaker. Tragedy is converted into epic as their seven voices interlace, creating the complex lyrical texture of *Thereafter Johnnie*, whose closest conscious literary parent is John Milton's *Paradise Lost*.

## Publication History

Thereafter Johnnie was first published in hardback by Random House, 1991

First United States softback, Vintage, 1992

First United Kingdom hardback, Virago, 1992

First United Kingdom softback, Virago, 1993

Second edition, softback, through 1stBooks, 2001

http://www.1stBooks.com

Excerpts from reviews of Carolivia Herron's

# Thereafter Johnnie

\* \* \*

—from The New York Times, June 23, 1991, John Bierhorst

"Carolivia Herron's fascinating and highly original first novel belongs in the distinguished company of Alice Walker's "Color Purple," Toni Morrison's "Beloved" and Gloria Naylor's wickedly satirical "Linden Hills." Profoundly human yet larger than life, these books—each in its special way—balance the unspeakable and the spiritual, adding a mythic dimension to the experiences of African-Americans.

"Thereafter Johnnie" is an accomplished, lyrical piece of writing that is also passionately intellectual...One of the characters in "Thereafter Johnnie" describes the story as 'a mythological narration of incest and national identity.' A young woman named Patricia, beautiful and amorous, makes love to her two sisters and openly desires her parents. Above all she craves her father, John Christopher Snowdon, a heart surgeon at Howard University, where his three daughters are students. Patricia, the middle daughter, has a affinity for the classics and a Joycean appetite for languages, and does briefly become her father's lover after he becomes estranged from his wife, Camille.

"...The folkloric quality of the tale is unmistakable, and it even rubs off on the story's locale, Washington. As I read, I kept reaching for my street map as though I were rediscovering James Joyce's Dublin.

"...Ms. Herron's style can best be described with the resonant term Matthew Arnold applied to Homer: "rapid." She frequently strings several short sentences together without punctuation, using the repetition of key nouns to maintain clarity and creating a style that is verbal quicksilver.

"...The guilt that nearly destroys the Snowdon family wells up from the corrosive, deceitful myths of racism and clashes with, and is finally overcome by, the healing mythologies of Europe and Africa. Genesis, Revelation, the Grail legend, spirituals like "This Little Light of Mine" and African-American folk tales like "The People Could Fly" all are woven into the narrative.

"...Like myth itself, "Thereafter Johnnie" does not provide a neat ending. Rather it offers possibilities; the struggle goes on. With its broad sweep, its

vii

complex imagery drawn from Old and New World cultures and its pervasive tone of universality, it is more than a saga of black revitalization. Part vision, part parable, it is a story for all America.

*The New York Times*

*   *   *

—from The Boston Globe, April 25, 1991, Patricia Smith

For weeks after touching upon the last trembling noun of Carolivia Herron's unsettling novel "Thereafter Johnnie," one is still a captive of her sparse and startling language. Each page pulls away more of life's pretty but complex packaging, and the truths beneath are designed to stun. Herron's raw poetics give hurt a new face—and the reader is drawn deep before realizing that the face is perilously close to his own. By then, the novel's stark and beautiful structural rhythms have made it impossible to pull back.

Johnnie, the child of an illicit coupling between her mother and grandfather, spends her childhood in silence. Unanswered questions seem to have burned her voice away. Her tortured mother, Patricia, whose every breath is tenuous, provides the only solid presence in Johnnie's life. Although their souls are linked, their purposes are not—soon after Johnnie speaks her first word at 17, her mother heeds turbulent voices and walks stoically into the Potomac. But that is not when Johnnie's life begins or ends.

Herron writes with the flask and unpredictability of random thought. One moment we are inside the head of the infant Johnnie, who watches as her mother seeks joy and pain beneath the hands of "grandfatherfather"...In the next moment, we are swept into the tangled rationale of the father...In yet another moment, we are pulled, flailing, into Patricia's obsession...

And we are with Johnnie, we are *inside* Johnnie, as she shudders to life, the truth bearing down on her, each revelation building instead of breaking. Thanks to Herron's impeccable weave, Johnnie is the thread that gives the fabric of this novel its somber hue and its strength...

"Thereafter Johnnie" is written in classical epic mode of 24 books, each with its own inevitable chill. The narrative switches tone, mood, perspective, and the reader hangs on, an addict to Herron's anguished rhythms. Comparisons to Joyce are inevitable; the author's sense of epic is evident (Herron directs Harvard's Epicenter for the Study of Comparative Epics), and her prose—and point of view—know no charted course.

Although we know early on what will happen to Patricia, and where Johnnie's search will lead, we want to see each wrenching scene played out; we want Herron to toss us about with a series of stark astonishments. There is very little in this novel that does not disturb. Happily-ever-after notions of black middle-class family life are shattered again. The world grows progressively crazier as Johnnie stumbles through her own story with no idea what she'll do upon encountering those words "The End."

...One shouldn't expect the world to be right again once this book is finished. Remember how a fever breaks. It heats, cools, toys with the system. And it won't let you go without a fight.

*The Boston Globe*

\*   \*   \*

"The tragic vision has been generally absent from the hopeful, Utopian literature of the Americas. A few poets—Vallejo—and novelists—Faulkner— have dared to challenge the American view that things will turn out well. But history and happiness seldom coincide. Carolivia Herron adds family and religion to the tragic conscience of American society. But she does it in a splendid way, by creating the origins of the Black communities of the New Work, their epic resilience, their clear-sighted disenchantment, their prayer for a time to heal, a time to transform experience into knowledge. Let me salute Herron's achievement: the creation of the origins in order to have a future—even if it be a tragic one."

—Carlos Fuentes

"This book is fated to be a groundbreaking work in the Afro-American and American literary tradition. Herron has managed, through a structural conceit that itself approaches brilliance, to bring the reader face to face with whisperings of our darkest thoughts and desires...I think it ironic that critics at large have been bemoaning the fact that American literature has produced no counterpart to James Joyce in vision and structure and that such a person has now appeared within the ranks of Afro-American literature. This is a book for the ages."

—Gloria Naylor

"An indisputable work of art...its powerful style and language, sometimes street-wise, sometimes biblical, compel the reader to continue."

*San Francisco Chronicle*

"Extraordinary...At once descriptive and meditative; a blues lament, a rap...[Herron's] novel explores the politics of race and gender in an uncompromising light. Thereafter Johnnie is true to life in the way that dreams—or nightmares—can be."

*Newsweek*

"Its formal intricacy balanced by an unyielding interiority, *Thereafter Johnnie* is a remarkable achievement. Herron sweeps into our literary tradition like a fourth Fury...and leaves very few things untouched."

Henry Louis Gates, Jr.

"Thereafter Johnnie is a bold and brilliant novel which tells of the fall of a family, the discovery of incest, and the birth of a child: Johnnie, the daughter of an incestuous union between her mother and her grandfather. More boldly still, it turns their tormented union into a strand within a larger tapestry of abuse whose origins are a sold as slavery, and whose consequences are nothing less than apocalyptic. Johnnie's is a story passed down through generations, a swirling and terrifying epic. It works out a vision of national damnation as inevitable as the House of Atreus...stunning and incandescent...luminous and visionary."

*Los Angeles Times Book Review*

# Thereafter
# Johnnie

For Sister Pamela Ann Smith
Janice Schuh Okulski
And the Villa Nova
*When Shall We Three Meet Again?*

*How doth the city sit solitary,*
*that was full of people! how is*
*she become as a widow! she that was*
*great among the nations, and*
*princess among the provinces, how*
*is she become tributary!*

**LAMENTATIONS I:1**

# Vesperus

NOW she is a light flitting through the halls of the Old Carnegie Library. They closed it down, then gave it to the University of the District of Columbia. They stopped having classes there. The black folk left, went up into the Allegheny Mountains when the war started. She gets brighter as evening comes on.

Now she is a light brightening out of nothing in the Children's Room of the Old Carnegie Library, out of nothing, because to a light there is no need for a way of getting there, through the front door, or through a window, or up from the basement stairs smelling of urine on days when the mild vagrants sat in the park. Down there damp they urinated against stone and cement. The door is locked. No one comes this way.

Now she is a light, Johnnie, henceforth and forever a light who walked and grieved the holy city alone now a light in the Old Carnegie Library, writhing in the Children's Room, on the second floor, a wincing aching gyre of light that whirlpools nothing into itself, there is only light in the light, only light. She moves out of the Children's Room into the hallway, leans first to her right beside the high display cabinets, then ahead a step upon the marble floor touches the doorposts of the room on the other side quickly, and then waiting, keeping there, a pillar of light beckoning, beaconing to no one, a light hesitating above the doorsill of the Science and Technology Room, no, not there, this is not the place, she whispers to herself, my mother never sat in this room, she glances away, she

1

returns again to the Children's Room, curves the separating wall to the Young Adult Room—she fidgets with the tabletops, a light. Johnnie.

Now she is a light, after all she endured to know, a castaway light waiting again at the door of the Children's Room, yearning, watching, hesitating before descending, she fumbles with the vanished books that fall from her handlessness.

> *Mary Cary*
> *Eight Cousins*
> *An Old-Fashioned Girl*
> *Curious George*
> *Pollyanna*

Touches but cannot hold. Grieves. Turns. Children's Room. Young Adult Room. My mother is not here. Nor here. Whispering light she descends.

Descend. Descend dear Johnnie, light-years away from us now groping against the carved marble posts between the floor and the top edge of the bannister, sliding to touch the wall beside the window. Down. Johnnie, descend.

Where are the young voices murmuring over thick pages when my mother was a child here reading at these tables? A voice of light whispering, which is no voice at all, only light. She steps into the hallway and to the marble stairway. Evening comes darker. Down the stairs, past the first floor to the basement, where once there were art pictures stored in a crowded room. To the left the Music Room, empty now, she huddles her helpless brightness close against the absent tables, Johnnie, hopelessly bright where she sits in absent chairs with earphones that have passed away and listens, a listening yearning light,

o yes now this little light of mine

Alone. Completely.

I'm gonna let it shine

A flickering light trembling flitting in the Old Carnegie Library at Seventh and K streets, Northwest, Washington, D.C. Washington City.

This little light of mine

Johnnie.

I'm gonna let it shine

2

Whispering through earphones in the basement in the Music Room, she hears the voices of the choirs of Third Baptist Church.

This little light of mine

Fifth and Que Streets, Northwest. Beat heart Africa flowing down Seventh Street to the Old Carnegie Library.

I'm gonna let it shine

And among the voices, a voice, a child's voice, her mother, Patricia, from the Tiny Tots Choir.

Let it shine, let it shine, let it shine.

Filling the space

> This little light of mine
> I'm gonna let it shine.
> This little light of mine
> I'm gonna let it shine.
> This little light of mine
> I'm gonna let it shine
> Let it shine, let it shine, let it shine.

In the Old Carnegie Library, empty now, except for a light. It is evening.

She moves in the hallways. A light.

They are singing at a church picnic. She aches and flashes helplessly toward the fried chicken, greens, potato salad, bread, rice pudding, butter cake, sweet, sweet, sweet candied yams. She smells the bitter metallic of the silver polish as the deaconess at the table inside the window prepares for tomorrow's communion. While the children in the gravelly yard are clapping and singing, preparing for celebration, she is a frantic light, gyring now on the second floor of the Old Carnegie Library. Frantic because the picnic ended long before she became a light.

Now she is a light condemned to perpetual restlessness in the marble halls of the Old Carnegie Library, Johnnie, in the empty city, holy, where once at the Washington Hilton there was a knock on a door, and her mother, Patricia, answered that door, and let enter that father who left Johnnie mute, voiceless, Johnnie who only wanted to rest murmuring as a child murmurs to sleep, now sleepless forever, who walked under the impotent sun until she became a whispering urging light.

3

Johnnie was given eternal life and immortality and heaven. Eternal life and immortality and heaven but she did not want immortality. She did not want to live. She did not seek to add life to life as I have added life to generation bringing this ancient song to you through so much time from my foremothers, no, Johnnie did not want another life. She did not want to be born again. She wanted to lie down and sleep. Just lay herself down in peace and sleep. Sleep. She did not want heaven. She did not want a land where she would never grow old. She did not want to see Jesus. She wanted to lie down in a bed and rest, and sleep, and cease. Johnnie longed for an end but failed to escape eternity, she was cursed with unvarying wakefulness, she was condemned to eternal consciousness, she was a perpetual flame in the empty skull of a vacant library, yes, she failed utterly and became a light.

Patricia as a child stood at a window watching a hurricane. In a great storm you are apt to think of the West, heartbreaking forests where Wyatt Earp or Davy Crockett stride above treetops. They shrug away the branches and drowned birds where you, Patricia, are lost and afraid, on Sixteenth Street, in the second-floor window. The western heroes hold a staff and stride through the treetops so high, where your body breaks, Patricia, watcher of forest storms, deserter deserted, Patricia. Grew up looking at the trees in Rock Creek Park. Grew up and deserted her child who became a light. Grew up and walked into the Potomac River, sent Johnnie racing from Georgetown to Washington in the rain in the afternoon. I escaped, left Patricia drowned and young Johnnie to Washington City.

This is the story. Sing of how it happened. I sing of how it happened.

Because now she is a light and cannot die. Johnnie. Who never wanted immortality. Alone in the city, alive, who wanted to die forever, who wanted without a dream to sleep forever, condemned to eternal life.

She knows she is a small dark space in a small dark box in an empty city at the bottom of the sea in drought.

She does not know that she has become a light.

a light

4

# The Last Time

HE is John Christopher. She is Patricia. He knocks on the door. She opens to him. This is the day and he is the father who leaves Johnnie mute. Today. Yesterday Patricia called from the Washington Hilton to John Christopher at Freedmen's Hospital. What? Yes! There is an emergency here at the hospital. Can she wait until tomorrow? Yes, Daddy. Tomorrow. She'll be all right.

From her suitcase Patricia takes the faded nightgown that her mother, Camille, bought for her own wedding night and took with her one afternoon in 1949, twenty-two years ago, when Camille rushed from her aunt's house to be with John Christopher to marry him. John Christopher wanted Camille. Camille never put on that nightgown. She kept it. It was not faded then. There was a sheen upon it. It was a blue nightgown with white lace. Never put on. Kept. Patricia heard them love whispering. How lovely the gown was then. Now, how lovely. Keep it. We must keep it where it is. Camille. How lovely with her wedding nightgown where it is. Love giggling. Mommy and Daddy loving and giggling a long time. Patricia took it. Patricia arose and stole the nightgown from her mother. Kept. Kept it. Hid it in diverse places. The rest of her life. Patricia.

She takes it out at the Washington Hilton. She hangs the faded nightgown in the closet. Blue. Bathes herself. Bathes Johnnie. It is a sunny day not very cold why not go out? Kisses Johnnie and kisses her more. It's not very cold. It won't hurt you, no. We're going to be all right, Johnnie, it's all right. She dresses herself. She dresses Johnnie. Dresses for a sunny day that isn't so cold.

5

Connecticut Avenue bends southeastward with noise with movement with joy with light. Stands at the window. Full of people. A city full of people. Patricia looks down through the city the heart.

Patricia walks through the room walks to the door walks out of the door turns around locks the door places the key in the bag on her shoulder pulls it up on her shoulder rests the bag on the white rabbit arm of her coat pulls on the brown leather gloves touches Johnnie. Reties the strings of her white rabbit fluffy hat. Steps outward. Thus. Brown boots on heavy carpet kelly green. Elevator, down flickering lights out of the elevator brown boots step out. Heavy royal blue carpet receives her brown boots step out on it out to it and the porter moves quickly to the door and the concierge moves quickly to the taxi stand and the taxi driver leaps quickly behind the wheel and the cab moves quickly to the door and the concierge opens the cab door quickly quickly and the driver quickly looks back over his shoulder as slowly slowly slowly slowly slowly the young lady Patricia holding Johnnie in her arms enters the taxicab, slowly.

She says "Dumbarton Oaks" and he's off quickly through the avenue quickly for the excursion Connecticut Avenue to Dumbarton Oaks to around with through along between in among beyond against about until they reach Dumbarton Oaks quickly quickly where slowly the young lady Patricia pays the fare.

She walks to the pool in the amphitheater. Many years ago when Patricia was a child her mother brought her there alone without her two sisters Cynthia Jane and Eva and she stood clustered comforted with other visitors listening to be told that once there had been concerts in the summer. There was a shining paper to describe it. Patricia remembered it. Sunlight striking a glazed brochure in a hand between ivy pillars swearing that once there had been concerts in the amphitheater of Dumbarton Oaks that was so eaten away now with grass and ice and ancient mud washed up beneath leaves cracking the bricks with gray water. There were once musical concerts German lieder and readings from Ibsen plays. Not anymore now. Once. Rarely. Sometimes. Even when Patricia was a little girl it was a long time ago when there had been concerts. That was almost before everything. That was almost the beginning. The amphitheater is not like the surrounding gardens but is unkempt, complicated. There are entwined bamboo and evergreen and autumn winter trees so that at all times the leaves are thick the steps crumbling the smell aboriginal mold for Patricia, a holy place secluded a place final as a sea with raw chill and blank decomposition to damp mulch, a place to go after seeing the other gardens but this time she comes to this place the amphitheater first, not last, with baby Johnnie.

She stands awhile and thinks by the pool brooding. Thinks and broods until dampness is melancholy and bamboo rustles between her and the city until evergreens rustle in darkness autumn winter trees wrestle whistling with emptiness. Abomination of desolation. She stands awhile and then after a while

6

that is enough. Enough. She rouses herself from melancholy to walk the path to the wild place, the fence separates the formal garden from the public park and the remnants of excluded black shadows the evicted dark peoples of Georgetown murmuring shadows, grieving muttering when she comes to the fence she turns and climbs the slope to a narrow path with low hedges, thus she walks into the north side of the rose garden Patricia stands there a moment. February. Desolation. Perdition.

That is enough of the garden, Patricia is cold. She walks out of the first gate and around the corner and into the museum and it is the best museum because each thing they have is set up all by itself alone. She stands with baby Johnnie in front of each thing each thing is all by itself alone. Patricia has returned many times Patricia has stood here before during many years and bright visits but before this there was no sadness and no Johnnie. Limestone and gold and jadeite and shell and serpentine and onyx and parchment and bronze and niello and ivory and wood and copper and bloodstone and silver all by itself alone and all by itself alone, a porphyry rattlesnake St. John of Patmos cup, vial, chalice, grail. All by himself. Alone. Holy Cup Vial Chalice Grail Urn Skull Cup. Alone.

Blurring darkness to light the tall glass panels between the gardens on one side and the exhibits on the other make Patricia dizzy with beauty. Patricia is dizzy with beauty. Johnnie. Patricia sits on a bench thinks about beauty until dizzy beauty becomes euphoria. Patricia is very euphoria except euphoria shines too bright in Patricia's eyes and becomes headache. It is enough. Patricia wants to go.

Patricia stands up and begins to leave touching the sales rack *Guide to the Dumbarton Oaks Gardens* if only there were something left to know. If only Patricia did not know already where everything is if only Patricia could need a *Guide* Patricia walks the long way to Wisconsin Avenue finds a cab "Take me to the Carriage House" Patricia is hungry the driver stops at the Carriage House Patricia isn't hungry takes Patricia back to the Washington Hilton Patricia goes back Patricia goes up thus, to Patricia's room, takes the clothes off Patricia's body and the underclothes and bathes herself and bathes Johnnie, again. Patricia sits by the window and looks out on the darkening city drink, drink, Johnnie, drink ringing down to have dinner brought up with a smile Patricia does not eat. Patricia sits smiling on the city while holding baby Johnnie cold in Patricia's arms it is so cold and dark. Patricia stands up and lays Johnnie on the other bed. Patricia walks to the cart and pushes it into the hallway. Patricia. Patricia. Lies listening in bed to Patricia's city, Washington, throughout the night and arises still listening by morning. It is the city of Washington it is dawn.

Bathes Patricia and Johnnie. Dresses Patricia and Johnnie. They sit by the window and wait a long while and then a short while longer and then no while. It is the afternoon. It is the knock on the door. It is Daddy.

"Daddy?"

"Pat?"

Focus on it. Look at it.

"Hi, Daddy, come on in."

Clearer. They are both in the room now, she is turning and turning to show him her new dress.

"prettyPat, yes, there you are again. My dearest patPat. How good you look! I expected the last rose of summer."

I look at them as they dance. I look at them bubble blue in gray dark water. The bubble is before my eyes, focusing.

"I'm fine, Daddy. I'm so glad to see you. Daddy, look at the baby."

Their faces approach the seam of thin film that encases the bubble in which they dance. The bubble swirls toward my face. Their faces approach my face, Mommy, and the father who takes away my voice.

"She frightens me, Pat, no, I won't touch her. So that's my child? Mine?"

He trembles leaning to me, then back.

"She's a beautiful baby, Daddy, our baby, ours."

He winces away from me. Ours.

"Beautiful, Pat? She frightens me so. Why does she look like that? Why does she look at me like that?"

"It's because she's so black, and her eyes are white, she has Ma's eyes."

"But Camille's eyes are green, with some brown. This baby's eyes aren't green, they are so blue that they're almost white and her skin is too dark for those eyes."

"It's because she has them open so wide now, she's trying to drink you in with her eyes. But sometimes her eyes are calm and look like Ma's eyes."

"I don't like to look at her."

I am cold I am pressing myself deep toward this bubble. I am cold, who has plunged me into this sea where I am perishing except for this bubble of air toward which I thrust my face.

"I love the baby and I plan to live here with her in Washington."

"Do you, my dear?"

"Yesterday Johnnie and I went to Dumbarton Oaks and we were happy."

"Yes, my girl, prettyPat, but come here to me a moment, I will do something for you."

"What is it?"

"Come over here to me my darling and let me see you naked standing in front of me. I want to see you naked again."

"What?"

"And I'm going to do something nice for you, I've planned it, I want to show you something prettyPat."

"Are you going to take your clothes off?"

"No, ma'am."

"You can't make love to me if you don't take your clothes off."

"I'll do what I want to do, sweetheart. I'll do what I like and you'll like it too, I promise you. Aren't you mine? I'll take care of you. Do what I tell you to do and undress sweetheart."

"You're not going to hurt me Daddy? Because of Johnnie?"

"No my dear, precious, not that, I won't hurt you. But my darling you must come here to me, sweetheart, come here to your father. Come and stand here, right here in front of me and take your clothes off. I want to see you completely naked again and I want to look at you, look as much as I want to look. You have chased me unmercifully. Aren't you the same child who has chased me unmercifully all your life? You have sent me to hell, dear heart, my sweet child, you have condemned me to hell. And yourself? Are you in hell too my Pat? prettyPat? But I own you my dear, I own you. I can do what I want with you now. Come here now and do what I tell you to do. Come. Stand over here with me right now my darling and take off all of your clothes for me so that I can see you.

He is the father who takes my voice. He has his will with my mother, and I, Johnnie, am compelled to see it, to know it. My mother stands before him and undresses herself as he sits and watches, gazing at the beige-brown flesh uncovering. I am the mute infant propped on pillows on the other bed as he sits and watches her royal blue dress, the starched ribbons and glistening lingerie in powder blue, navy blue shoes, sway of breasts as my mother pulls off her slip, knees and pale thighs rising above a puddle of blues.

"Your underpants too. I don't want you to have any clothes on at all."

"Why? I don't want to take them off. Why do you want my clothes off? Why do you want me naked? Are you going to make love to me again? I'm afraid of you, Daddy. I don't know what you're going to do. I don't know what you're doing to me. Will you make love to me again? I want you to make love to me. I don't trust you."

My mother kneels before him in the soft puddle of her blue clothes and pulls down and off her last covering, from her waist, over her hips, from her dampness to her still silent feet.

"Come over here now darling to the bed, and let me do this for you. Yes come on and yes a sweet kiss just like that, yes, lie like this. Relax for me, open your legs and relax, that's right my darling, I want to touch you and speak to you."

So as it was in the beginning, the very beginning, as it was in her infancy, he places his right hand between the legs of my mother, and I watch carefully, carefully. Yes my eyes are open and they are open still keeping the blue clarity in front of my face of the father who takes my voice this day this moment and my mother whispering, "Daddy," and gently the merciless father who takes my voice pulls together the lips of my mother's sex, his daughter, I see it clearly I will not

9

forget what I clearly see pulls the lips of her sex together and pulls in rhythmic motions toward the curly dark pubic hair of my mother so that the soft inner flesh massages his daughter's my mother's vagina and then moves up in insistent soft patterns to the tender flesh just above her vagina right there and farther warm to the base of her clitoris my mother's where he presses the sides together slightly, still not touching his daughter's clitoris directly but urging with his brown fingers on the reddish flesh of her sex and then without touching the tip of his daughter's clitoris my mother's moving his hand down again to caress her vagina, the walls of his daughter's vagina, her cervix her womb, through the delicate motions of his fingers caressing through the pale skin the darting flurries of throbbing hesitating blood that recognize his fingers, flow to the touch of his fingers. He urges his daughter's sex softly softly again until he sees the slight undulation of the deep muscles of her thighs my mother's thighs lifting to the throb of accelerating blood rushing toward her abdomen right then he stops the rhythmic motion for a moment using her soft flesh to form a cushion around her clitoris a palpitating steamy tenderness in which her clitoris trembles and stretches for what it cannot touch right then with the tip of his fingers he softly pinches the tip of her clitoris and releases. And begins again the rhythmic motion.

She does not strive or struggle because he is taking her there in his hand and she does not move her hips and she does not pivot her muscles and his five fingers coax her desire and lift her up and carry her and he sees the rising color on his daughter's face and neck, rising.

"Daddy?"

"Yes, Pat?"

"Daddy?"

An infant girl child may lie upon a bed unblinking as a sea edges the carpets an infant girl-child dressed warmly enough so that the cool of the rising hesitating sea casts no disturbance before its slow uneven rim of water an infant girl-child unblinking at the hand of a father between the legs of his daughter may not notice may be incapable of recognizing may have no fundamental faltering in the region of the chest as the innocent water touches first the tables and beds, his hand there, an infant girl may see only his hand and that just seeing that onlyness that not noticing the ocean that losing of voice not before the profundity of the sea but in the face of a gentle male hand on open female sex that unconsciousness of the sea, will it be an encouragement? "Daddy?" "Pat." "Daddy." Johnnie. Encouragement for the sea to come on in? Come on up? Arise however slowly? "Daddy?" "Pat, prettyPat, precious, beloved, darling, come to me." "Daddy. Daddy." "Yes."

And as for that ocean, as for that great water, how would it know itself? What would it do if such a thing were to happen that while an infant girl-child lay unblinking at the hand of a father between the legs of his daughter while the sea came under the door quietly, what then, what would such an ocean be thinking of? and would it be the last sea? would it last forever? would it finally dry into desert? wind swirled world without end.

"Daddy. Daddy. Oh, Daddy!"

As it was in the beginning.

"prettyPat, my darling."

"Daddy."

As it was in the beginning, is now, and evermore shalt be.

"Yes, come to me my darling. Come."

"Daddy, Daddy."

"Yes."

Swirled without end, Amen.

# Faerie Tale

*ONCE upon a time my mother loved my father but my father left my mother one early morning in February. He left her gifts of money and jewels but he left. So my mother took the gifts of money and jewels wrapped them and kept them, wrapped me in a blanket. My mother put on her hat her coat her gloves she held me in her arms she came down from the penthouse of the Washington Hilton. Her heart was broken.*

She finds she rents a room in a house in River Terrace with a porch that looks toward the Eastern Branch of the Anacostia River and from there we hear the nearby intersections of roads, waters, electricity, telephones, bridges of Minnesota Avenue and Benning Road. She withstands late winter. Snow comes hard late to Washington City this winter. Her days are one continuous day within which she steps an ice skater between the walls. Cracking. Losing balance. Collapsing. Falling upon the frozen floor. She tries to sleep. The blackness beyond the icicles keeps her awake. She lies on her stomach, her elbows bent. Both slightly cupped hands against the mattress. Terror and the soft pillow at her side. My mother, Patricia. A murderer comes, breaking through the lock and shattering the sliding glass door he stalks to her bed and slits her throat. I watch. She raises herself up trying to focus upon him. Nothing. She pulls the comforter around her head. Icicles pierce the air beyond the glass, hung tears. Only it is too cold for tears unless a freezing thing should cry as it died, unless a toss of warm Atlantic seawater should arrive suddenly at Arctica, dropping so late so fast upon

Washington City this winter. Icicles gather light into stagnant flame, glance through sparkling glass and white white curtains, icicles clear cold like my own eyes, my white blue eyes in my coal black face looking at my mother my eyes, elongated, distorted, multiplied along the rims of the eaves of the porch imprisoning stalactites of cold vision my eyes, empty, crystal, terrifying eyes, out of blackness. Crystal, as crystal as the polished Venetian glass bird the one my mother loved and broke in her anger once, a frozen crystal river encroaching upon the sea, the sea.

"Daddy, Daddy." As if there is hope. As if he presses his cheek in the warmth between her neck and shoulder. She is delivered up to the altar of sheer absence, given to the white walls who answer her whimpering calls with that exact despair from which her soul cannot recover. "Daddy, Daddy," brown velvet eyes "Daddy, Daddy," I see those brown eyes open on the room, she seeks him upon the wall dust, casts her yearning upon innocent walls, "Daddy!" It can happen, yes, it can happen. Those lovers never to be seen again have returned. They have stomped at last through the doors of the forsaken. There have been knocks on doors. It can happen, "Daddy! Daddy!" and anguish leaps as a stone leaps against the seawall in Cinquetera south of Puerto Escondido on the Pacific of México leaps to her throat, breaks her head, cracks her face, rips through to the sheet, tears holes in the mattress, shredding, unleashing—she leaps from the bed, crashes hard against the wall, her head hard, the wall, the wall, out. Then through the glass porch door groping, groveling the drifted snow on the brown wooden floor of the porch beneath the icicles screams, screams once—brushes off the snow calmly and the dirt, smoothes the puff of her hair comes calmly back into the room. She washes her hands, she smoothes her hair, she returns to her bed. Some innocent, it is probably some innocent who has been murdered. How much it must hurt to be killed. My mother hears the young, high-pitched wavering cry of a child who casts such a long cry upon the air, it must be that it has been murdered. There have been murderers there have been betrayers who murdered little children burned them up thoroughly drenched them in oil and set fire to them or left them naked on hills to freeze and starve or cracked their unknit skulls upon stone cement or stabbed them or raped them or fed them to wolves. Fed them to the wolves. I have seen the wolves. The wolves come quietly over the frozen Anacostia River. They come at sunrise and eat the children.

River Terrace Apartments. Water. The Potomac River the Eastern Branch the Anacostia River. There are shelves of ice sculpted from frozen mud. The sun is bright mist filling cold air. When the air is so bright it is hard to see. My mother cannot see. Sunmist. The absolute directed act of light upon matter. Sunmist of vision, my mother, the unveiling of objects. There are blank holes in the sidewalk upon which she walks. Her eye focuses on a small white stone. Her eye imagines it on velvet under glass at Dumbarton Oaks Museum. A small white stone the emblem of her enchantment, it means nothing and yet she cannot move another

13

step she cannot move she cannot see. A small white stone singled out as the milestone of the indistinguishable moment beyond which her mind cannot go, no, no further, her mind, no further. This, this is the moment she has been waiting for, my mother. Monomaniacal. Thoroughly insane. Beyond return my mother. She sees a white stone in Dumbarton Oaks Museum under glass and sticky fingered children peering over railings at it. A white stone washed up or down the water courses, deserted remnant of lost oceans, small featureless skull. A white stone on the sidewalk at River Terrace beside the Eastern Branch of the Anacostia River before which my mother falters.

The beauty of torture, the delight of slavery, the joy of being tied up bound down whipped beaten drawn quartered stretched broken into the ground is this— the mind is free. Is this, this, there is no way out, giving up is simplified. With warm flesh in shreds, limbs broken torn, guts lashed slashed hung hooked, body held down trussed up bent over, skin fingernails toenails stripped off, breasts cheeks ears eyes stuck stung pierced, feet palms knees elbows shaved and shaved again to the bone, limbs pinned open spread askew separated detached, genitals mauled, split, sliced, eliminated it's easy, so easy, so finally and absolutely easy. It must be endured. In such extremity the impulse toward life, living, is uncomplicated, smooth with minimal variation. It simply must be endured. That is all. It must be endured. There is no escape. There is nothing that can be done. The mind can rest. After so much perturbation, so much weighing of possibility, so much consideration of choice, opportunity, alteration, adjustment, coercion, influence, reversal, reconsideration—nothing. Nothing can be done. The mind is free, free, free indeed. Free at last. Released from complications of survival, from the necessity to devise its own release, caught then forever, in flame, tarred and feathered, castrated, raped the mind discovers infinite stillness—there are no decisions to make. It's just like love.

My mother stands on a sidewalk in River Terrace, I am in her arms, she looks down upon an arbitrary white stone. The afternoon light is hard. She wants to go back to her family on Sixteenth Street. She wants to leave Anacostia and return uptown. She wants to see Janie at the convent. They have all turned from you, my mother. What will you do to save your soul from the terror that slices through sunlight scattering the air the wind the sound of the traffic frightening everything away my mother what will you do what shall we do my mother my mother while the light cuts down so cold against us my mother this terror that will not stand forth clearly in this terrifying light but scatters shatters in the eyes breaking into fragments of glistening ice slivers of light, my mother, lost, holding the scream within your body against me I feel it what shall we do?

Frantic. You cannot stand here looking down at this white stone forever. You must move at last, and when you move what will you do? You do not know how to save your soul. You will die with this unbearable grief around your heart battering at me through your body. I feel it. You are utterly alone except for me, a baby in your arms. You cannot go home. If you could only receive enough sun inside your chest my mother, you could be a princess, you could dance in a golden skirt and your heart would not be broken. Your heart is broken.

And maybe after a while you could learn to do other things, my mother. You could learn to play tennis or swim or drive a car. And what if you really do belong in the world after all and the prophecy is wrong that says you must lose your soul? Why should you lose your soul? Why does so much horror lie upon you? Why don't you give up and live? like my Aunt Sister Cynthia Jane and my Aunt Eva? Why should you be daimonic with dreams and prophecies? You don't want to die, you want to go home.

Janie, Janie with the other nuns doesn't think of Joseph. She has Mary and Jesus, she doesn't need Joseph. He was a lonely boy to grow up and marry God's wife and daughter, Joseph, the visionary sinner, king of adulterers, avenger. Incest. He thought he was chosen, he was a child pariah, brooding, skulking against the walls of the temple when they spoke of the hope of Israel. He thought he was the one. He thought the sunlight was on him.

Later, nauseated, in his trade, wondering, wood shavings sifting through his fingers with thoughts, he saw the virgins passing his door, Mary. What of Joseph? Patricia, my mother hates the world and does not want to be in it. Hated. Did not want to be in it. And I am tired. I have been telling and telling to you this story from Washington City and I don't know where I am. Where is Washington City? What has happened? Why can I not see? Is it a flood that has washed away the city and am I caught behind a flood that has washed away and dried? I? Am I speaking from the depth of the sea, or has the sea receded and do I speak from a dark box cast up upon drying sand? Is there sand where everything was? Where is the place where my mother and I walked before I came to this dark marble box? I will not see them again, my people, Washington. So solitary, that was once full of people.

I am telling a story the story of my mother's look and her loveliness and me. When she woke up to me for my mother it was like falling asleep.

*Once upon a time*

*Once upon a time my mother loved my father but my father left my mother one early morning in February. He left her gifts of money and jewels but he left. So my mother took the gifts of money and jewels wrapped them and kept them, wrapped me in a blanket. My mother put on her hat her coat her gloves she held me in her arms she came down from the penthouse of the Washington Hilton. Her heart was broken. She found she rented a room in a house in River Terrace while winter ended. She took a cab to Diotima in Eastland Gardens. Diotima once at the Benning Heights Community Center once when I was held within my mother's body Diotima had been kind. My mother found her again after I left my mother's body they drank tea while Diotima fell in love with my mother and my mother did not fall in love with Diotima.*

Diotima looks from her window in Eastland Gardens. We are coming. What is it? A branch budding quietly? We are coming. The cab bringing us moves as a glittering sliver between slices of light, thin, substanceless as a curve of dust in the slant of a venetian blind, or protruding light through a tear in a curtain, or sheer light. We are coming. My mother stands with the sun in her face, holding me, stricken, Pietà reversed, the stricken mother over the grieving child who is me.

Diotima enters the room bringing tea a steaming teapot two cups a bronze tray. Diotima steps upon the floor mats, they flatten beneath her steps and lift back. Diotima sits across the table from my mother. My mother leans against a large pillow, white with small orange flowers.

A flickering speck at the edge of vision A branch budding quietly. It is spring.

A tea leaf floats a slow circle in my mother's cup. My mother moves her hand almost plucks out the speck, a torn tea leaf does not pluck it out, lifts the cup instead. The screens between the rooms are beige with gold leaves. The leaves are raised as in brocade. The light in the room is sharp, the light leaves my mother and me in shadow. The crystal table takes fire from the light, Diotima floats in brightness and shade. She is not beautiful as my mother is beautiful. Mottled light waves on the screen behind Diotima, and where the screen has been left open the shadows, tree shadows, limbs, dance on the woven mats.

A flickering speck at the edge of vision. What is it? A branch budding quietly?

Diotima turns her eyes between mother and child. Touch, Diotima, touch the rich color of my skin, caress, only a flicker of fingers on hand my mother's hand, your fingers caress, but touch the rich color of my skin black dark black coal black night black ebony black polished black anthracite black pearl black midnight black tar black macadam black onyx black touch, but caress my mother the desert color, sand beige dry, and with the circled fluff of hair gentle, gently touch her, my chill, freezing, not burning but frozen desert mother.

"I thought I would return to my family by now. I thought this would not be long. Now I know they will not take me back. My father has given me money and ordered me to leave Washington, to leave the United States in fact. He feels that as long as I am anywhere near him I shall hurt his career as a doctor. He says I destroy his skill by needing him too much. I shall never leave. I've been studying where to hide here in Washington, I've decided on Georgetown. Help me, Diotima, please help, I can buy a house in your name. He won't find me. I cannot leave Washington."

"Buy a house in Georgetown? But what about black folks? In Georgetown the black people are almost all gone. We would be alone and what if your father or one of your father's patients should see you there anyway? To hide from him you won't be able to go out. They would recognize you. You would never be able to go out at all. You would be so sad. And you would get sadder."

"Yes, I know, yes, I've looked at it, I want it. I need rest, I need to rest for a while. In Georgetown there is space with no one in it, there is no one I know nobody I recognize and no real D.C. black people, in Georgetown the Potomac River is calm, I can rest with Johnnie, and with you Diotima if you help me. We can buy a house I could stay there with a window with the Potomac River a soft chair gold velvet and rest my sadness in peace."

"But Georgetown! Georgetown. I've never wanted to live away from a black community. I never have, ever since I left México and came here and had to live around gringos, in México we blacks were just Mexicans like everybody else, my father couldn't take it here and went back. White people up here don't want us in Georgetown and why should we want them? Why can't you live here? There's Anacostia, Kenilworth, Eastland Gardens, Deanwood, Parkside, Mayfair, Capitol Heights, River Terrace, Langston, Benning Heights, there are so many neighborhoods for us here."

"I can't stay here, Diotima, I'm going to leave Anacostia I hate Anacostia, I hate Kenilworth, I hate Eastland Gardens and Deanwood and Parkside and Mayfair, how I hate Capitol Heights and River Terrace and Langston and Benning Heights, I hate Anacostia. My mother grew up in Kenilworth everybody who has ever known me walks through Kenilworth all the time, my family is known too much around here and I can't stay here.

"I'll live in Georgetown Diotima where nobody ever hurt me I was never hurt in Georgetown I want a place in Georgetown as far as I can get west in Washington as Anacostia is east. I want a tall house on the Potomac my father has given me money I could be there you and me and Johnnie all three of us. I've thought and thought. We can do it. Let's get away from here. Let's get away from the Eastern Branch. Let's get ourselves together and go, hidden above the river and send out for everything. Every afternoon Johnnie and I shall walk by evening by night by fog by the water by the Potomac. In the winter you and me and Johnnie shall gather ourselves in from the cold. We shall have a fireplace. I'll have a place to rest my sadness." She stands. My mother stands up with me clutched in her arms.

"He has made me swear I shall leave the country he doesn't want me here I shall not leave the country or the city the money is contingent upon my departure you could help me with your family in México you could divert the money he won't know where I am. Help me, Diotima, help me, help me. We must find things to fill our house, we must find furniture and dishes and rugs and the chair, the golden velvet chair I want so much, I want to sit in it Diotima, I want to sit in it right now and when I look out of the window I don't want to look at Anacostia, no, never, I hate it here, let me get free let me go let me out of here and everybody who's not here is up on Sixteenth Street or North Portal Estates I've got to get out of here Diotima help me, help me Diotima we have to move we have to move fast get the house ready fast it's April I have to be there fast, fast the house must be bought and prepared and filled before autumn Diotima I'm telling you you've got to help me please help me Diotima. Diotima. Help me Diotima." Her language halts, the flow cuts off, then softly, "I can do it, we can do it, believe me, help me."

My mother pauses. Pauses again. Diotima is afraid. What is it? What has happened? Diotima looks at my mother's entranced suffering body. I am forgotten, cramped in one arm, the left arm, while she lifts her right hand in a gesture rising in repudiation, a gesture with which to cast off all relationship, a blue satin cloth in that hand, presumably for me but not mine, not mine, blue satin sky and her right hand rising in a gesture that is her signature, higher against that sky, no, no I shall not have it I don't want it I shall not take it if you force me to live I shall tear down your life, says that gesture of utter repudiation what does it portend my mother? "I do not want it, Diotima. I want no part of this world. I shall have no part of this place. This Anacostia. Let me get to a place another place where this place this Anacostia this Kenilworth this Mayfair this Eastland Gardens becomes the other place, that place, another place where I am not, where I never come. I shall not be a part of this ground. I shall not live as it lives. I repudiate it and I ask you to come with me away Diotima," her lovely hand her beige brown arm lifted upon the pale blue sky of the cloth held high casting away the clouds of heaven my mother my beautiful beautiful mother in horror as she holds me against her beige marble breast, a sculptor's breast, smooth, perfect, classic, the curve of her legs beneath swirled lavenders and blues for spring, spring swirling within the eyes of Diotima, my mother's exhausted arm uplifted, held, my mother, Diotima, their eyes meet and Diotima stands up. In that silence. "What has happened? What is so wrong? What has made you so unhappy?"

"Yes, you see, I'm probably insane. But I must hide somewhere...he has almost killed me. I don't have a home. My head hurts I've been raving all the way let me have my house."

*Once upon a time my mother loved my father but my father left my mother one early morning in February. He left her gifts of money and jewels but he left. So my mother took the gifts of money and jewels wrapped them and kept them, wrapped me in a blanket. My mother put on her hat her coat her gloves she held me in her arms she came down from the penthouse of the Washington Hilton. Her heart was broken. She found she rented a room in a house in River Terrace while winter ended. She took a cab to Diotima in Eastland Gardens. Diotima once at the Benning Heights Community Center once when I was held within my mother's body Diotima had been kind. My mother found her again after I left my mother's body they drank tea while Diotima fell in love with my mother and my mother did not fall in love with Diotima. Then we all moved to Georgetown and*

18

*after a while they deserted me and escaped into death and homecoming, and I, I alone, lived unhappily forever after within the struck diamond of Washington City.*

# Journal

### APRIL 3, 1971

I love you. And there is silence after I write these words on the page. I am surrounded by nothing. The city dissolves. The baby who has been with me, the house I cannot see around me. I love you. There is a pattern to the days to hold in so much, to keep me from dying. I know now that you do not desire to go with me when I go. I understand. And if I am too distraught to sustain the pattern, I have at least a recurrence of habit, when the placement of my body in the room recalls old necessities, and so I wash my face, and smile into the towel or I turn back the spread at night. Why am I not gone? I should be gone. Memory is a lemon rind caked with salt in the day of famine and drought. How I love you.

An image of the sun interrupts me, brown and yellow landscape of the desert I imagine, and that interrupted again by the scent of a florist shop, the cool breathing of refrigerated roses, and then again, the sunlit desert. And these images are of you, somewhere in this city. Rubbing your face against my mother's body. You are more free than I.

A journal written to no one. Written because I am trying to find a way to live. I am a weak searcher. My strength is gone. I want to see you again and know how it feels again with the light dusting your eyes in that particular green sunlight of our garden. This is an awful life to live. I don't want to live it. Come with me again, and go to bed with me and please touch me again.

It could be a surprise if we turned toward each other in that sunlight in the garden, and you would see how beautiful I am. It would brighten your heart for you to see me again. My beloved. This page will not fill without me. The words stop. Will you ever lie with me again? How gentle you are to me when your fingers are soft on the front of my body. I should not have touched you in the beginning. I should not stay in this city now. I love you. Do you remember me happy? When you got me the apartment on Kalorama Road two years ago I thought it was because you would be my lover. But you wouldn't be my lover. I had to work so hard to get you to make love to me and I wanted so much to have a baby and so I got pregnant. But then you made me move away from there and you wanted to give me an abortion. I've been staying in places throughout Anacostia since then—River Terrace and Capitol Heights and Eastland Gardens and the Benning Heights Community Center, where Johnnie was born.

You used to like me so much and the shadow was not on your face then, and you leaned toward me and sometimes came upon me suddenly and held me but I did not know your heart. Your love was only true in the sunlight but not in your heart. And what you meant with your hands upon me and when you lay with me and when I opened my legs and you touched inside me is something so different from the way I understand. And I was caught. I started it. I found a way to touch you first and now that I want to sleep with you I cannot. I can do nothing to save myself, I cannot leave this city.

You and I went to Dumbarton Oaks and I stood on a stone bench and laughed and you turned toward me with the light above us. You came to me and lifted your arms as I stood there, O God, and your fingers touched me softly, soft. You teased me with your fingers and told me that love would stop you, love with me, the kind of love in which we would lie in a bed together. You told me that you would not, would never sleep with me, even as you swayed me with your arms lifted to me, and your fingers touched my breasts. And then looking up at me you lifted the skirt of my dress and brushed the hem of it against the back of my leg and lifted it slowly. You put your hand under my dress slowly and so softly, and lifted the skirts of it, and the back of your fingers touched my thigh, and I felt your hand there, I remember. I remember. It happened. Once upon a time it happened. You, the person I most desire in the world have touched me with a gentle gathering hand and you felt me so warm as I am there. It's true.

I love you. You walked over to me slowly in the sunlight and lifted my dress. How warm the sunlight above the dark thick public garden on that path that winds down from the grassy circle with the smooth parallel trees and the shallow cool fountain, down from the rose garden and the grape arbor and trellis, and the small darker fountain with the quotation from Dante dampening the cove where I sat with baby Johnnie, here in the winter, it was just a short while ago, since you left me. But it was a long time ago when the sunlight was so warm and the dark rustling voice of the public garden rose whispering around us, and you were

21

ashamed and happy because you wanted to kiss me so much, and you did, or almost did, it was almost the best time, but you stopped before it was over and I remember how sad it felt for you to stop. With me still standing there. I wanted that kiss. You never liked to want to kiss me. You were ashamed when I pleased you. You did not want that kiss.

How is it that sunshine always mixes with all that is a premonition of departure? What makes horror so bright? The light shines brightly to tell me to remember, remember. I am marking the outline for myself with light and filling the space so that I may see. I look and see what is before me and see that it is large and grand and tragic and even the gods have known about it and see how hopeless it has been for me to shield myself or try not to fulfill what was spoken of me, because here it is, the moment that was foretold, the event of my life, the one trouble I was born to accomplish and not survive in this world, the horror from which there is no escape, because my task, the task of my life, the path I walk to complete the destiny of my life, calls down the curse of heaven through my hatred of this world. Repudiation. I have imagined myself, have your eyes not seen me? from the very beginning, high and tall against a northern sky, gesturing, denying, turning away toward black cloudy heavens above the city. I am lost. You stopped kissing me before the kiss was over. I leaned toward you and brushed just the tips of my breasts against you. I never got used to it, your moving away from me. Never.

I am unloved. And the purpose of this journal is to probe out of the innocent paper, a response, an answer, a secret language to interpret and own and finally recognize as a handful of blood smeared and dried irregularly on the paper. The blood is an event I remember, dipped from the warm bowl of the heart. Rubbed over the fingers, considered. And then you wiped your hand on your doctor's cloak.

How I would welcome sleep. Sweet sleep. What is the way out of here? There is no way.

Now there is an explanation of my dream of the tower and how I stood upon it. I was high and grand and they called to me from the ground saying, "Come down, come down to us." And they wanted me to be among them, and I had chosen to be among them but when I stepped upon the air to descend I was already gone. I stretched out large upon the air, first northward and then turning eastward, southeasterly across the Atlantic Ocean. There was dust singing from that water, O wade,

> Wade in the water,
> Wade in the water, children
> Wade in the water
> God's gonna trouble the water
> Fly away black bird

You ain't never gonna fly
Fly away black bird
You ain't never gonna fly
Cause your momma's name is lonely
And your Daddy's name is pain
And they call you little sorrow
Cause you'll never love again
So why you want to fly black bird?
You ain't never gonna

fly away home I heard the song and the brown specks of my body dissolved into the air, flickering at the edge of vision and I was gone.

The image had come to tell me of this moment of this helplessness.

And that ocean is always calling to me, raging and calling through the corridors of the great rivers. My nightmare is that great ocean. I have seen my skull lying in that ocean.

If you had only understood how much I love you, you would not have left me. You would have touched me forever. You would remember forever your eyes traveling down against my body, sweet hesitating eyes full of consciousness and joy, waiting for me. Waiting for a moment to take me, to ask me, to persuade mc to come to you.

I must leave this world. I want you to go with me. I have been allowed one to go with me and it is you. I shall return and take you.

You are the father who gave me being. Whom should I desire but you? Whom should I possess? You will return with me to the other world of light and joy where we may live at ease among the gods where I shall sit beside you, the queen of heaven as you are the king, and I shall be your darling and your daughter forever, although in this world you have deserted me whom once you thought so lovely. Blessed is she whom thou hast desired never. Cursed be she who has been loved of the Lord. Who can please him long?

# Monopoly

CAMILLE leans smiles warm she is warm between her hips and shy across the table leaning her lips toward his face. She pulls away inward jumps breathes her eyes away from his eyes he almost leans back toward her but not quite she almost follows him but holds herself she wants to touch herself, stops. She stands looking downward, "What is it, Chris?"

"One hundred dollars for Oriental Avenue."

She is sitting down again, buys it, places the money in his hand, smiles he pulls her fingers, teases quick heat pours up her arm from his fingers trembling her arm her shoulder itches, she dips her cheek toward her shoulder pulls her hand away. He stretches out his hand toward her. The deed of Oriental Avenue. He brushes the edge of the deed up the underside of her breast. Again she leans toward him, whimpers, lifting her hips from the chair. He places the deed of Oriental Avenue in front of her. Neatly.

"Just visiting in jail."

"Why is it always my turn?"

"You have to kiss me since you're in jail. Lean over to me and let me have some mylady. Kiss me or you forfeit the game and you'll have to lie down for me sweet right here in the floor and open your legs, you can't be shy it's just a game we're playing, yes, come to me any way you like, hide your face if you have to but kiss me."

"I don't have to kiss you."

"Yes you do. Do you know that I'm going to sleep with you tonight? Tonight I'm going to get you. I'm going to get all of you, you're going to give me everything. I'm going to have you, I'm going to be holding you when it happens." His hand holding her fingers.

"Ono, Chris." Heat again, heat swirls up she pulls her fingers from his fingers. Heat pricking the skin of her stomach and up across her breasts. "Ono."

"It says here you owe me ten dollars."

"That's not fair! I keep owing you everything."

"It's just a game. You have to play by the rules of the game."

"You make up the rules, Chris, why can't I make up a rule?" She presses her thighs against the chair, raises her hips upward, heat again itching, burning, she twists, startles upward between her legs, she drops her head, whining, whispering to herself frightening new passion, "What is it? Do I like this? Is this good?" "Is what good?" he hears her, "Ono I—I itch down there a little bit, Chris. I don't know." "Does it feel good?" She looks to the side, twists her body toward the window away. "Does it feel good?" "Yes, Chris." And the heat startles up again and she raises her body, her hips again and turns her head away.

"What are you doing to yourself? Look at me when you do that, don't look out of the window, don't be ashamed, look at me, yes my love look at me when you feel that feeling." Flashing and rippling across her face, heat, fire, "Give me your hand." Her fingers burn in his fingers. The quietness of her desire sends a small whimper toward him blushing, "Are you coming to me?" It is a small tender sound he barely hears her he smiles, "I know what you're thinking about mylady." "No." She tries but can't pull her hand away he keeps holding her hand, "Ono, Chris." "Yes." Holding on until desire rises from her abdomen outward she pulls away but can't get free from the heat until he lets her go. She holds her burning fingers.

"I pull you to me slowly mylady, my darling Camille, I let you go and I see you move your legs around and twist toward the window and whimper to yourself 'This isn't good' but you know it is becoming good for you and I'm moving toward you gently to get you, so that I can have you slowly, mylady. You'll he very sure that you want me."

Monopoly.

"If you want to make up a rule of your own you just have to apply to the banker." She is frightened and trembling and happy.

"Really?"

"Yes, really. That's all. Just go to the banker and mortgage some of your property and then I'm sure he'll let you make up a rule."

"What do I do first?"

"First you come over and talk to the banker."

"But if I do that you're going to touch me."

"Never!"

"Yes you are, you'll feel me."

"No I won't."

"You promise?"

"Absolutely."

"I don't think I like your silly game, Chris."

"Come and tell me why you don't like it."

So playing she comes to him and playing he pulls her skirt above her legs and sits her on his lap.

"Ono, Chris, stop."

"Stop what, I'm not doing anything. What do you want to exchange for a rule?"

"Oriental Avenue."

"I don't want Oriental Avenue."

"But I don't own anything else."

"Yes you do."

"See, now you're going to touch and play with me."

"No I'm not. That's against the rules."

His brown hand is warm beneath her skirt his fingers warm brown from the creased dip between her thighs toward her hips, she moves, she presses her downy orangebrown skin against his hand but softly, "Chris?" Deeper farther his fingers probe her hair.

"I want you so much mylady Camille."

She twists to face him, leaning her arms on his chest, "But what do I own?" her face against his face.

"Don't you know my love, mylady?" dipping, probing, "Don't you know what's yours?" His fingers are inside her, he pulls on her sweetfiesh, he holds her trembling.

"But if it's mine why are you touching it?" Softsweetly is held her hand she loves she can't hold back pull away but kisses him while his hand keeps and keeps her very well. "It's not yours my sweet lady Camille, not yours but mine to touch and to caress and kiss not yours but mine," gently he sweetens her he keeps and plays for keeps his game slowly to make her stake everything make her come after him, "not yours but mine but what's yours mylady? something is yours to keep or to trade.

"Stand up then my love, stand mylady and tell me what you want? What's yours?" His tongue almost touches her lips. When she moves toward him he moves back. When she moves back he approaches, she tries not to go after him, twists herself away but he does not let her go, he holds her, holds her burning fingers kneels, lifts her skirt, lowers the cloth the secret things beneath, lowers kisses kisses her fire, kisses his very own Camille his tongue toward his very own womb, caresses he scatters his fingers along the curves of her beneath there,

"Camille, mylady Camille what do you have mylady? something is yours to keep or to trade." He is standing now, turning her, coaxing.

"Show me, show me what you have, show me what's yours." She writhes for him but will not go after him.

She wants him the want is all over her "Oh Johnnychris" he is there opening her legs he touches her liquid he tastes "It's not enough," he says, "tell me what you have." She runs from him lies down for him but he, "Take off your clothes for me." Camille is losing almost everything, "What do you want mylady, tell me what's yours?"

Looking up from the floor taking off her clothes lifting her skirt "Please come to me please." He holds her between her legs holds her toward him, "What do you want? what's yours?"

"But it's happening in me now, Chris, right now inside me."

"It's not enough mylady Camille, tell me what you want, tell me what's yours? I love you, mylady, I love you so and you have to give me everything give it to me again and again because your sweetsex is mine and not yours, let me make you my wifelover and tell me what's yours tell me what you want?"

"Johnnychris, I'm having an orgasm right now!"

"It's not enough mylady, it's not enough, tell me what's yours.

"I'm so hot, so hot Johnnychris, how can you not come to me now, I want you to come to me come."

"Nono mysweet, you can't stop now, give me everything, come highhigher you have to show me what's yours."

"My legs are weak, I'm lying here for you, get down on the floor with me and kiss me I love desire you Johnnychris I'm soft and warm and open and I want you inside me sleep with me lie with me put yourself inside me I want you."

"No, it's not enough you have to show me what's yours and let me see what's mine turn over and let me see you from behind and touch what's mine there and kiss you there yes but show me what's yours this isn't enough what's yours mylady, what's yours? I own you I own your body now you show me what you own and show me what you want to do with it I'm not going to do it for you because it's yours."

"Oh Johnnychris I ache for you come to me come oh so much I want give me," and weeping at his trembling body, weeping, reaching, "this is mine, I'll show you" unloosens his belt, unzippers him she pulls weeping down his pants and love she touches "this is mine, this" pulls him down hard beneath her twisting over him leaving on ignoring to take off his shirt his socks there right there timewasnot to finish she wants "but Camille?" she spreads her thighs over her very own penis smoothly in together John Christopher and Camille.

27

# Three Witches

YOU were not prepared for their circle or their dancing or that you would be so struck that there were three of them—you knew there had to be three, they are your children, your own daughters, you knew you had three daughters and yet you had not considered the strangeness that they were three, you had not imagined them mysterious, you had no way of knowing until you saw them dancing in a circle—they danced violently in the snow singing, there was even moonlight, you could not defend yourself, yes, there was moonlight and snow and dancing and singing in a circle, when you found them unwittingly and brought them home.

Your first thought is to break the circle. They were singing and clapping and dancing a black song you never taught them they must have learned it somewhere—a black song that tried to be religious but mixed with vulgar words, at Camille's church they didn't sing those songs, and part of it sounded like a dirty street song black children sing, but they had never been on those kind of streets, they weren't supposed to look at one another like that, were they kissing? they should have known better than that. It is not possible that they did not know those kissings if they were kisses were too close even for sisters, and surely if they had been girls who were not sisters those kisses between the words of the song were not, were not respectable. When you first took Camille for your wife, and you had children together, and you fathered these three daughters, you had not imagined that they could think of rubbing against one another like that, were

28

they touching one another like that? it was impossible, you had not imagined they could kiss. Did they kiss? You had not expected it. If only you had known it was possible you could have planned for it.

Your second thought is the admission that they do not love you. Their problem was not, as you had believed, not that they loved you too much, but that they did not love you at all. You knew their affection for you, you stood looking at them and recalled their teasing and playing with you—but all those small pettings and cajolings that had occurred between you and your daughters were absentminded caresses to pacify an old fool of a father when compared with the fondling, probing, interconnecting arms and bodies you saw playing in a circle in the snow, and their faces were close—you could not see clearly from where you stood but surely you saw kisses—they weren't really kissing one another were they?—no, they had never loved you. They were playing and touching one another, your three daughters. They loved one another. Why had they never treated you like that? as one of them? Whenever you had played with them swinging them in circles they had jumped up and down all around you calling you, Daddy, Daddy, Daddy and you had chosen them one at a time and swung them until they giggled and giggled and then you would swing the next one, but had they ever, all of them, danced in a circle together? You could not remember that they had ever danced together like that. You were nothing. Their small kisses on your stubby cheek in the evenings had no meaning beside such antics as these you saw playing before you in the snow, your three unruly daughters.

You thought they loved you too much, you were prepared to wean them from you, you were going to teach them as they grew up how to do without you how to change their affection from you to their boyfriends, you thought you were doing it right, but there they were dancing and singing in the snow in the moonlight in a circle that night when you went to bring them home. They had forgotten you. You were nothing.

There had been no need for you to walk from the hospital to the upper campus of Howard University that night in the snow to find your daughters, it was already arranged, you were to wait in your office until they finished their meeting, their poetry reading, it was black poetry this time, not regular poetry, black poetry they said to you, mixed black poetry that mocked and teased regular poetry with black rhythms—is it possible they listened to it? that they wanted to listen to it? that they had ever heard it? that they recognized it when they heard it? how did they know the words to that song? how did they create it? they created that song themselves using black poetry and black music mixed with regular poetry.

How could they have learned it without you knowing that they had learned it? You didn't mind them knowing it but you minded not knowing that they knew it, wild black music, why didn't they tell you? why didn't they ever let you know they liked that kind of music? where did they learn it? and who taught them to touch one another like that? were they really touching? and were they kissing? Whatever it was you saw them doing, you knew you had to stop it.

You believe that you were innocent then, but that they were not innocent. You could tell that they were doing something strange—you couldn't see well from where you stood but didn't they want to make love to one another in bed with their clothes off? You believe that's what they wanted, they were not innocent. Maybe they had already done it to one another, how could you know? And what did they do in bed to make their dance so exciting? Maybe they weren't doing anything, it was so hard to see, but the dance was so, so exciting and lively. You wanted to be with them. You wanted to know what they were doing. You insist that you did not interrupt innocent young girls who were just playing and dancing and singing and growing up. If you had waited in your office you would never have known, you would not have seen what they were doing. Why had they pretended to love you? all they wanted was one another. You were a fool.

You thought their love for you would make it hard for them to grow up, because of their attachment to you, their father, you worked hard to be the best a father can be to his daughters when they are growing up and wanting things and you wanted so much to be the one giving things to them so that they would know that their father is good and you took good care of them, you watched each one as she was growing up so you could be there tearing down barriers whether it was some racist teacher at school or if they needed more money or clothes in a different style so they could be unique—there are times in a child's life when a particular brand of shoes or a jacket with a special label means so much, those times are so rare in a child's life when their wishes are so easy to grant and mean so much to them and you wanted them to know how special they were, and different, and you gave them all of these special things, when the other children were going to expensive summer camps that had nothing special about them except they were expensive you didn't just choose camps that cost a lot of money you put thought into it and you sent Eva to be a junior apprentice at a newspaper and Pat to a camp for kids who were good at languages and Cynthia Jane went to tennis camp—you worked hard to find special ways for each of them to be special, you tried to create a world for them in which they were so very different from other children.

You were sitting in your office trying to work but you were worried about them and the poetry reading should have been over or perhaps they were still talking and discussing and if you went to meet them you would hear part of it and figure out what made the poetry interesting for them, but you found out that the reading was over and there they were playing in a circle and singing and playing in the middle of the campus in the snow in the moonlight—nothing stranger has ever happened to you in your life, no, not even when you were a little boy and that chicken pox vagabond came over to where you lived in Atlanta, came over

30

from those swamps in Savannah and frightened you so bad when you were a little boy, they were touching and playing in the snow like three maniacs, three witches, three weird sisters—your own daughters. They were supposed to come down the hill directly to the hospital to meet you after the talk was over, but they hadn't started and they weren't hurrying you could have waited all night. If you had waited they would have been calm when you saw them again you would never have seen them dancing in a circle and singing you would never have known.

Your third thought is that the City of Washington is beautiful. Washington. On such a night you turn back to look out over the city from the top of Howard Hill, Washington by moonlight, a bowl of white silver light under night and snow and moonlight that slants above the lab buildings the cold is pleasure on your cheek and in the grating sound of your steps on hard snow. This afternoon has been almost warm for a while, now there are black spots in the street, how dark they are under moonlight spaced out by snow, black where there has been melting but now frozen can you feel it, John Christopher? snow and cold and ice, snow and cold and ice and the crunch of your boots, regular, comforting, even, going somewhere with intention, up. Your footfall beside the Psychiatric Building, up, the speckles in the wall of the Architecture Building glistening by moonlight. Beside and around the dark brick Chemistry Building, you glance at the covered tomb—squat building at the base of the hill, aslant from the Pharmacy Building and across Fourth Street toward Mary McLeod Bethune Hall, Sojourner Truth Hall—quiet, then you walk up the left side of the grand ceremonial stairway that embraces the silent hill leading up to Founder's Library.

Now Washington is behind you, John Christopher. Step carefully, listen, the cloth of your pants rustles as you lift each leg, up, your coat opens and closes, you crunch your way to the top, mighty sinner, now turn, turn, turn to the city, the great city sitting in its bowl of visible white light darkness. Washington. Clear black and white shining.

Look. From the southeast to the southwest a clear line, Kennedy Stadium, the Library of Congress, the Capitol dome, the spire of the Washington Monument—all transparent with marble light shining through. Howard Hill, Howard University Hill descending on your left into the McMillan Reservoir and the Washington Hospital Center and East Capitol Street and the Catholic ghetto plains of Turkey Thicket with its nunneries and convents and monasteries and seminaries and Catholic University and the Shrine of the Immaculate Conception, Immaculate spire and dome curving at last to that other dome and spire of the city, but first the hill dropping on your left toward the Arboretum and the Anacostia River, down, down to the Tidal Basin, the Jefferson Memorial, the Lincoln Memorial—and in this cold the memory of cherry blossoms icy in your nostrils, Washington, and on your other side, to your right the hill dips to Georgia Avenue, little Africa, then rises to Cardozo Hill, where they shot Mr. Clifford for

31

making peace, rises to Clifton Terrace, higher still, where the black children and their jump ropes and balls and jacks and bicycles are one day to be the last and only protection left to the great city, John Christopher, for the day will come when black children leave Clifton Terrace and on that day the city shall surely die the hill continues westward curving, leaving the black folk, dipping into Rock Creek Park to rise higher still north of Georgetown arcing through the golden bowl of the city, the bowl overturned to form a transparent dome of pale perfect light held up by the spires of the Washington Cathedral, the highest point of the city, holding up the sky to keep it from falling and interrupting the sweet memories and the rosy delicate murmurs of St. Alban's School, Sidwell Friends School, and The American University, from thence the hill curves down toward Georgetown, stopping for a moment at Dumbarton Oaks, shuddering before descending to the Potomac and the Tidal Basin and southward toward that sea where so many of our ancestors lie fathoms deep. So many. Fifteen million black Africans undone by death. You stand at the center of this first dark footfall of the Allegheny Mountains, circumscribing the city on the east and on the west and in the north, with the Potomac River itself on the south. Washington City is a dark cup of white light.

There is a black circle protecting you behind you the liberal arts buildings of Howard University and the Miner Building, the oldest building of the University of the District of Columbia. And also Rankin Chapel. The African Studies Complex. The Administration Building. African-American Studies. The dark pinnacles of Miner Teachers College intruding. Douglass Hall. Crampton Auditorium. The Stadium. Ira Aldridge Theatre. The Fine Arts Building. The Student Union. Education. Literature and Home Economics. Languages with Astronomy on top. Environmental Studies. The Undergraduate Library. Founder's Library. Rankin Chapel. You stand between Founder's Library and Rankin Chapel. Turn and pray. Why don't you turn and pray it's been so long since you've been to church with Camille and your daughters. Stop right here now and pray. You are alone, there are no footsteps in the snow, you need a long perfect prayer because this is the moment, the ancient curse that follows you out of the south arrives again tonight. That thing you have most feared has come upon you. Tonight. As in the beginning. If it were not too late, you could just walk to the chapel, but the abomination of desolation is already with thee and the torment long foretold is engraved on the chapel window, dark-stained window glancing with oblique light a muted last judgment, Woe to the Inhabitants on Earth!

You heard Pat scream with laughter behind you on the wide upper campus Pat and Janie and Eva were playing in the snow laughing and screaming, Pat was running and laughing from one side with her arms spread out leaping jumping, Janie shouting and running to meet her cutting diagonally from the other side, Eva leaping just to the right of where they met, on top of the snowy picnic table,

32

dancing in the snow clapping her bare hands in the snow, screaming, all three of them screaming with laughter, you were frightened, Janie and Pat collapsing into each other Eva with a spray of snow flinging between them all three of them in a whirlwind of tossing snow scooping it up into the air twisting in it catching one another's arms and dancing in a circle surrounding the table sweeping off the table with their arms beating their hands, their bare hands against that cold table, then Janie found some sticks and started hitting them together in a wild irregular beat while Eva swayed and turned and turned and turned singing, Janie and Eva were singing while Pat went around them in a circle making snow angels lying flat on her face in the snow making angels in a circle so many so quickly leaping up falling down frantically until the angels seemed escaping demons leaping down and into the earth from their frantic circle.

> I got wings o lordy
> You got wings o lordy
> All of God's chillen got wings
> When we get to heaven
> Gonna put on our wings
> An' gonna fly all over God's heaven, heaven
> Everybody talkin' 'bout heaven ain't going there,
> Heaven, Heaven
> Gonna fly all over God's heaven.

Your fourth thought is that always there are stories of three witches and the fourth is always a king who is betrayed to his death. You were the king. They were the witches, girls, daughters, your daughters. The king must be killed through the power of the witches but if the king could overcome the witches he could save himself. Salvation. That's something the chicken pox vagabond told you when you were a little boy. He explained it. You looked at your daughters. How long had it been, John Christopher, since you had lost your last chance for salvation? On that night you doubted everything, you doubted yourself, you doubted what you had always wanted for your daughters. You discovered that you feared something about them and you wanted power over them, you felt the terrifying warning of that power in the fire that stirred upon your thigh. You were in hell, it was hell, this stirring of the fire upon your thigh at the vision of your daughters dancing, you could not escape. You could not escape because you desired them, you wanted to be with them, you wanted them to include you. You could not bear to see them dancing there without you apart from you, they were not thinking of you, John Christopher, you had no part in them although you are their father, it wrenched you to see them free of you and you had an uncanny fear for your life. They were daimonic. Separate. You could not bear it.

You could not do it, you could not maintain yourself before these three Furies, three Graces, three Fates Pat turning handstands along the inner edge of the angels her thick winter clothes falling and laughing laughing jumping up and Janie hitting the sticks together and Eva beating on the table and Janie's song louder and louder and the part of the song you could understand was an old spiritual,

> I got shoes o lordy
> You got shoes o lordy
> All of God's chillen got shoes
> When we get to heaven
> Gonna put on our shoes
> An' gonna walk all over God's heaven, heaven,
> Everybody talkin' 'bout heaven ain't going there,
> Heaven, heaven
> Gonna walk all over God's heaven

and Eva shaking her body and beating on the table and singing along with her or humming "aaahh" on one note while Janie was finishing each phrase, Pat down on her knees coming in with a frantic soulful jazz rhythm, and then the part of the song you couldn't understand

> Momma made a bundle in the bed last night
> Momma made a bundle in the bed
> Momma made a bundle in the bed last night
> Momma made a bundle in the bed.

down up down up not with the melody but almost attacking changing the melody,

> I got wings
> I got a harp, o lordy. I got wings
> I got a harp I got shoes

clapping

> How she make the bundle in the bed sweet chile
> How she make the bundle in the bed
> I've got a song o lordy
> You've got a song
> All of God's chillen got a
> Momma makin' bundles in the bed.

some black street song mixing and messing with the spiritual and it seemed to you that they weren't singing about heaven at all, not about heaven, but about hell and death, your own death, a curse, there were words you could not understand, Janie standing beating the sticks together singing with her full open voice Eva standing on the table clapping her hands slowly as the song moved fast breaking your heart, her song broke your heart, she rose higher, catching up Janie's melody and Pat's low jazz rhythm she took them away, took them higher, took them away from you singing,

Heaven

her voice let them escape,

Heaven

they escaped through her voice,

Everybody talkin' 'bout heaven ain't going there,
Heaven

their circle rose higher and away

Heaven
Momma found a bundle in the bed last night,
Momma found a bundle in the bed.
Momma found a bundle in the bed last night,
Momma found a bundle in the bed.

and you feared there would be no breaking that circle.

Gonna dance allover God's heaven.

There was no breaking that circle, not life, not love, not hate, not marriage, not death, not any alteration in this world or any world, as you saw them there together you were convinced that they were witches, three witches, and you believed they should never have been born to curse you, if you couldn't break their circle you would die, how was it they ever came together? you considered their sorcery an excuse, an explanation for what happened between you and my mother.

Before, at the times when they looked up to you, Janie and Pat and Eva, when you took them to a museum, or to a theater, or to the zoo, they clustered around you so happy. Daddy, Daddy, Daddy, and you gave them everything they

35

wanted because they were good and happy and because you wanted them to be special among the other children who were always crying for things, balloons and cotton candy. Your three little girls ate the cotton candy and held the balloons and walked near you through the carnival or the park. They knew that they were very special and completely individual and so precious.

Your three little girls. You read them stories at night you watched each daughter separately and so well and carefully so that you could understand and decide on their differences and encourage each one in whatever difference she had. You smoothed all the troubles from in front of them whatever they were when they were babies and when they were older so they could play and study and enjoy the things they liked best in the world. Your three daughters.

When the three of them were together and strong the rest of the world was dim and pale and turned askance its accursed ungifted head and wept for envy for longing desire for jealousy for hatred and you gave that to them, you made them high and precious and they were all you wanted and you wanted to be like that too. Filled with the power of the world, and you gave them that gift, that power, and then they left you out. They excluded you. They didn't want you or need you. When will they meet again? Your three daughters? When will those three meet again? Never, never again. Not since my mother stepped out above the Potomac River. They met on that afternoon, I saw them. But that earlier time when you saw them dancing together it was in the snow. Not in thunder, lightning, or rain. But in snow. In the snow a trinity and they had no room for you. They will never meet again.

You decided to break the affection among your daughters and pull all that affection toward yourself. Their soft humming floated to you over the snow.

Gonna dance all over God's bundle

but you could not allow that because you wanted to go with them too, and since you could not be with them you would try to overpower them.

And so you tried to turn them to you with your surgical magic. At the hospital they saw you lay a dog out on the table and cut out her heart and place that heart in a silver basin of ice water. Your daughters held the dog's heart in their hands. Then you placed the heart back into the dog again and brought the dog back to life. You lifted your fingers from the bloody ice water in the silver basin and you brushed your fingers against your white coat. You had done what you had sworn to do. And did you possess them then? Do you think this is the explanation for what happened between you and my mother?

Your last thought as you come to yourself suddenly is that you have not three daughters, not three, but four. I am the fourth.

# The King Of Hearts

ELECTRONS. Protons. Magnetic attractions. Impulses within the central nervous system. Movement. The soul is made of. Feeding on photosynthesis. Converted into flesh. This is incarnation. This is the kingdom of heaven. This is the truth. This is what is special about your Jesus. Jesus figured it out and told John, they figured out that it's everybody, all life, all flesh is the incarnation of light. The people who walked in darkness have seen a great light, and the light is the life of everybody. Including the latest thug drunk rapist they just brought in from Seventh and T. Light and magnetism and food made out of light. Listen to me. Food is light. Light is food. Blood brings that food to you. Blood. Blood comes from bone and is sent to you through the heart. I fix hearts.

These are my daughters. Janie and Pat and Eva. They are going to come later to the animal lab today. They are going to watch my experiment on the dog. Yes, they can take it. No, they won't get sick watching the blood. They'll like it, they'll learn a little something too. Why are you putting bad thoughts in their heads about my work? We'll be inside anyway. You should sit here and smile and type. Stop grinning at them so much. Stop talking to them. Stop talking about me to them. You are supposed to be taking care of the office. Any other day you would be all over the building spreading lies putting everybody's business in the street. I see you all over this annex and the main building too, spreading lies, when you're supposed to be taking care of my office. But here you are today. Of course. Anything to be nosy. Get out of here. Go somewhere. Let me talk to my daughters.

Look at the frog. This model frog I keep here on my desk. Have you ever looked at it? I know you've seen it before. I know you've played with it. But think about what it means about life and death. It means life is made of stuff. And death is made of stuff. Electrodes. The frog is dead. Electrodes make him hop and skip again. Poetry. Do you want to know where poetry comes from? Do you think it just descends from heaven through magic? Poetry. Configurations of electrodes. Dead or alive. When will you understand?

Let me tell you a story. It was a black surgeon who performed the first open heart surgery. That's him there, on my desk, a bust of him. He was tired of giving up, so he went for the heart and fixed it. He died when I was eight years old, that was when I got my power, I know it.

My office. Chattering. Secretaries. Disturbance. Stupidity. You never understand anything. You ought to listen sometimes, and think, or at least shut up so I can concentrate. Each human body has its own system. I think myself into bodies until I understand them. I know the ways in which an individual human body intersects with the ways of all human bodies. I know when not to fix something. I know when something that is wrong is supposed to be wrong. I cut deeply and neatly without waste. I sew bodies back up again. I can do it. I know how to read the signs. You don't know how to read the signs. You think the signs are in heaven. The signs are here in front of you and you hate them. You hate snot and slime. Snot and slime are signs. You hate spit and pus. Spit and pus are signs. You hate putrid sores and stink. You don't understand. You don't understand anything. You hate life. You hate human life. I love human life.

I gave you life. Life. And still you don't know anything. Life is a gift. Everything you think about has something to do with your body. Give life a chance. You could find out that you love life. Decide finally that life is worth it. Live it. I want you to live it. What could have happened to make you hate life so much? Why are you so sad? You read too much poetry. And you believe the wrong things about poetry. Poetry doesn't come from outer space. Poetry doesn't descend from heaven. Give life a chance. Life is stronger than the interpretation of life. A drowning person who is trying to commit suicide struggles to inhale air no matter how much she hates life. The lungs and the heart don't give a damn about her ideas. They want air. They want food. Life is stronger than poetry. Poetry. Poetry is made out of earth. There is no poetry in heaven, what do angels need with a poem? Poetry is human. You say poetry comes from the soul. Poetry. Blood, magnetism, darkness, division, perception, understanding, intelligence, the soul is made of.

Listen to me. Follow me. Watch. Come down to the lab later today and see the dog running alive. And come down again tomorrow when I will cut her heart out before your eyes. Come and look at her. They found her out on Seventh

38

Street, down on Georgia Avenue. Stray bitch. She is in my hands now. I will cut out her heart and strip it—I have to strip the heart and the pericardium in order to keep her body from rejecting her own heart. She won't even recognize her own heart when I am finished. But I'll give her heart back to her and she'll keep her heart and she'll live anyway. Do you want to learn to believe in life? Come and see. Watch. A golden bird you say. A sick rose. A forbidden apple. Poetry. Yeats. Blake. Milton. That's all you talk about. It took blood and a flesh heart to imagine the golden bird to interpret the sick rose to envision the fruit. I will sew the blood and flesh heart back into the dog. Your poets are made of the blood and mire that you hate. It takes heart. You gotta have heart. Blood. Life, yes. You say there would be nothing to live for without poetry. Without beauty. You tell me beauty is truth. You would not know beauty or truth or poetry without blood. There could be no golden bird singing prophecies upon a golden bough in a golden tree without blood. Your poet had a beating heart. You would not believe that there is nothing to live for without poetry if you did not have a heart. If you were in heaven you wouldn't know anything about poetry. Listen to me. I win, I am the truth. The world is good. Look. My fingers know where the blood goes, how to keep it going there, my patients lie down to die and rise up living. I know the truth. Heaven is empty. It isn't heaven, it's the sky. The sun and the moon are in the sky. That's all. Not in heaven but in the sky. Mind. Soul. Genius. Poetry. Truth. Beauty. Configurations of electrons and neutrons and protons. Life. I am tired of explaining it to you. Why won't you understand?

They are coming now. I hear the elevator coming up bring the full tray over here, is the pump primed? what? yeah, it's probably my daughters coming, my three literary geniuses, we're going to show them something today, yeah! It's a real shame! It's living with a bunch of poets, they call themselves Blake and Yeats and Milton! Hopeless! I've heard more about those damn poets than I've heard about dissecting aneurysms. Yeah, they love their poets. Blake and Milton I can put up with, at least they admit the existence of the body, but that damn Yeats! If I could only get my hands on him! Child looking me straight in the eye telling me that a golden bird on a golden tree has it all over real living breathing bodies! And I tell her, there wouldn't be any damn golden bird on any golden tree if Yeats hadn't had a muscle and blood heart! But she won't even get mad, that Pat, just laughs at me, you should hear 'em, always arguing with me about creativity and poetry, nuisance kids, every night I can hardly eat dinner without a bunch of poets harassing me, all evening they're at it, those three, telling me what life really is. Poetry. Life. Where was I anyway? Let me run through the rest of these things.

This is life. She lies there spread-eagle on the operating table, unconscious, the mask of anesthesia tied around her nose, her chest wall is open in preparation for open heart surgery. Here is the silver basin. Here is the stand. Here is the silver basin on the stand. Here is the ice. The ice is in the silver basin on the stand. The naked heart will lie in the ice in the silver basin on the stand. Follow me, come and see. My vagrant daughters. Where are my daughters?

Cynthia Jane. You keep looking for perfection and inspiration. What about my heart-lung machine? there is nothing equal to it, it loves life and hates death. You could give it a name. You could call it Jesus, Savior of my Soul. No, it's not blasphemy and I'm not making a joke. Do you think a muse is going to come leaping out of heaven just for your sake? You've been looking for inspiration in all the wrong places. You need something new, a machine that keeps us alive when we are dead. This is the whole works. This is where everything comes from. The rest is periphery, fingers, toes, tongues, extra, extravagance, the main thing is here, heart and lung. Not even the brain is in the center. The brain can rest. The brain can be unconscious. The brain can sleep. The heart and the lung go shunting on. You say the brain tells the heart what to do. You say the soul tells the brain what to do. The brain tells the heart what to do because the brain is fed by the heart. The heart is fed by the blood. The blood is fed by light, converted light. This is life. Life is pumped by the heart. The soul is nothing but light that feeds the heart that pumps the blood that feeds the brain that talks to the heart that moves you.

Patricia. You worship the dead. You read languages but you don't speak them. You don't care about them. You worship the dead. You manipulate abstractions. You pretend to be an ancient Greek because it makes you believe you are calm inside. You are not calm inside. The ancient Greeks were not calm inside. Nobody has ever been calm. Life is busy. And you're just faking it. It doesn't work. You are not dead. You are alive. Why are you looking at me? Don't look at me. But you don't even see. You don't focus prettyPat. What is the lovelook on your face? And why does it come and go so suddenly? Are you in love with me, prettyPat? Sometimes you look at me as if you are in love with me but that cannot be. And then you just sit and read dead languages and do nothing. What are you thinking, prettyPat? are you in love with your father?

Eva. The only one who has a desire for life, who welcomes it, but the others won't give you a chance. Polymorphous pervert. You are attracted to all life forms. I know. But they will tell you that you are the moon or some such rot. They will make you believe that no matter how much you involve yourself with life, you have escaped it. I have heard them talking about the way your fingers touch the grass, eternal virgin, renewing virginity like the moon. Isn't that what they say, your sisters? Negating your love of living things, grass and flowers, my unhappiest daughter. You love to make up stories about how people live, what it feels like to run through a garden, to laugh. You hide your thoughts from your sisters because they would desert you if they knew, if they understood. Come and look at what I can do. I will show you the core of life and you will be free of them.

40

Why does Janie look at Pat when Pat sits in the parlor chair, the gray velvet chair, Pat sinks into it and gazes through the windows with a blank on her face. Inarticulate. Stupid. Caring for nothing. Except she cares for me. She stirs things up. Why? What's the matter with her? She actually told me that she's in love with me, with me! Her father. But then she looks so bored and tired all the time. She's pretending to love me because she's bored. She's creating passion out of nothing. Why else are her eyes so vacant sometimes when she looks toward me even when she is saying that she loves me? She pretends to be in love with me.

Janie and Eva and Camille look at me strangely in the evenings because of Pat, but I have not sinned. Pat. I can't help it if she makes up this passion for me. It's not my fault. Their eyes on me. And your eyes on me. prettyPat you worry me. What is it? Don't touch me prettyPat. As beautiful as if you were my only child. But please don't look at me. Don't find me. I don't have a special love for you, Pat, I don't love you more than I love Janie and Eva and Camille. I love you the same. Don't touch me. You hate everything except me. You hate everyone except me. Your love for me is your desire to escape abstractions, to escape dead languages, to escape words. You want a real life. I understand. I will save you.

I'm tired. I'm tired of thinking about so many things, help me, Camille, I am in hell. Everything is all mixed up. Why do they mock me? Why does Pat, prettyPat? why am I in hell? Camille. You are silent in the garden, in the greenhouse with the gardenia. I want them to believe in me. What good is it to have created a whole world if they don't believe in me? Pat has no soul. Her love for me is an act of indifference. I can't get it out of my head that Pat has no soul. She doesn't care. My patients have risen from the dead for nothing. Camille why do you turn from me? I am in hell. Queen Camille. They laugh at me. My daughters mock my science, they tease my knowledge, they call me names, dream forestaller, interrupter, destroyer of the temple, Daddy, Daddy, Daddy. They say they are free with or without me. I laugh at their poetry and their freedom and I tease them about the life I gave them and I call them by the names of their poets taunting them. You, Blake and Yeats and Milton, all three of you have hearts.

The laboratory demonstration will illustrate the principles of extracorporeal circulation, techniques of open cardiac massage, cardiac fibrillation and defibrillation, and blood gas analysis, fibrous thickening of the leaflet, thickening and shortening of chordal tendineae, fusion of the commissures, rheumatic fever, arteriosclerosis, bacterial endocarditis, brucellosis, three literary geniuses. My three literary geniuses are here today. Blake and Yeats and Milton. And what else?

Massive pulmonary embolus is obstruction of the pulmonary bed to a degree that is life threatening and is associated with a drop in systemic blood pressure and severe anoxia. The statistics are rather bad. Nine percent of the patients live for twelve hours, fifteen percent live for six hours, twenty-five percent of the patients live for one hour, and the rest—well...massive pulmonary emboluses is a mother!

I understand trocar and cannula tracheostomy respiratory insufficiency mitral stenosis aortic stenosis patent ductus arteriosus pericarditis coarctations of the aorta tetralogy of Fallot atrial septal defect olord I understand but I don't understand the dance you danced and the song I understand the emotional disturbance produced by the prospect of the operation I understand precipitate attacks of acute pulmonary oedema I understand that in cases of mitral stenosis it is advisable to prescribe a sedative such as six milligrams of phenobarbitone twice daily for a few days prior to the operation it is also important to ensure sound sleep during this period by the administration of a hypnotic such as sixty to two hundred milligrams of sodium amytal I understand over transfusion may precipitate cardiac failure the patient should be sat up intramuscular injections are often poorly absorbed at first do not produce sedation and may be absorbed later when a further dose has been given producing the same effect as an overdose saddle emboli at the aortic bifurcation may present with color and temperature changes in the lower limbs with pain in these limbs and in the rectum this calls for urgent embolectomy the major mortality of the operation occurs in the theater with Janie and Pat and Eva penetration of the myocardium or passage of the needle through it into the right ventricle seldom produces any significant I don't understand Janie and Pat and Eva olord I don't understand my daughters they don't fit I understand hemopericardium but damage to a coronary vessel may prove fatal a large effusion may do using a sterile technique the vein or artery is exposed and a catheter selected the catheter is cleaned by wiping it with a swab dipped in a bowl containing two hundred and fifty milliliters of sterile saline the swab is discarded and the process repeated three times to remove the formalin in which the catheters are sterilized I do not understand Janie Pat Eva

Janie Pat Eva why did you dance that dance why did you sing that song what does that circle have to do with poetry the poetry is dead the poetry is for dead things but the dance you danced mixed up heaven and earth I don't understand

I understand using a twenty-milliliter syringe to clean the lumen by injecting saline through it the second bottle of saline is then poured into a clean bowl and five hundred units of heparin are added using the clean syringe the catheter is filled with what are you teaching our daughters about me? What have you taught them? Why do they recite so much poetry? Why does their poetry leave me out? What do they do to one another in bed at night? They all want to fly. They don't want to swim or run or something that is human and possible. They want to fly with just their arms. As if they had wings. They think that I don't understand. Do you think that I don't understand when heparinized saline is introduced into the vein? a light ligature around the vessel will prevent blood escaping during the procedure under screen control the catheter is then advanced until the tip lies in the right atrium or other predetermined site heparinized saline is injected throughout in order to maintain patency of the catheter Why were you singing that song? I don't understand. Explain this to me. Let me teach them, Camille. Let me try. Why should they hate life? I don't want them to love poetry more than life. And spirits. They aren't spirits. You know very well that they aren't spirits. And what about that song they were singing? how does that song fit in? They added something to that song. That song never told them they could do what they were doing how do you expect me to stay in here? There's no room in here. You are always in the greenhouse. I want my three daughters to love me. Camille. What do you think of our children? I've done everything I could think of. I put in a swimming pool. I had them put in archways in the garden. With roses. Lots of roses. Your roses. They are for you and my daughters. You have a greenhouse. You have morning light and evening light. Why don't you have any room for me really? Where is the heartbeat? patPat patPat My daughters, my daughter. Passion. Black hole collapsed. Collapsed upon herself. prettyPat. Something will happen. Something is going to happen. It can't stay like this.

I found you by a garden, Camille, I found you and loved you. You were sitting in front of the Student Union looking down at the reservoir. I was taking a break from the hospital. You became my wife. I built a house for you. I love you. Haven't I loved you? You are always so soft and lovely and you stay in the greenhouse. What are you thinking, Camille, what are you thinking about me? You can decorate the house any way you like. You can have a maid. You can go looking at ceramic vases. I don't mind, I like it, I make the money for you. I sew hearts into bodies for you. For you, Camille. What are you thinking about me? I have loved you long, Camille. What has happened to my daughters? Why are they singing African songs? Why are they always reciting poetry? Why don't they know the difference between African songs and regular poetry? They mix everything up. What has made them change? They didn't sing songs like that before. It's that poetry. Poetry makes them too excited and then they forget all about heaven and they want to make love to one another. I want them to forget heaven and love the earth but I don't want them to love the earth like that. No. Do you remember when I first found you, Camille? You had just started summer school to get a headstart on course-work for the fall. You had just graduated from high school. I found you and loved you. Camille, I am afraid. They mix up everything. I don't want them to love poetry more than they love me. When I teach them to turn away from poetry to love the world I don't want them to go to bed with one another. They mix everything up. All of you are insane because you hate heart and blood. If you hate and avoid and hide your attachment to the earth, chemicals, electricity, you hate yourselves. Do you worship poetry together? Do you think that worship has nothing to do with your bodies? Do you think that worship is spiritual? I can tell you that nothing is more unified than spirit and body. You talk about the poetic sublime. Ecstasy. There is a relationship between

43

ecstasy and sexual climax. You may not like to think about such things, but it's the truth. Be careful of the poetic sublime, you could end up in bed you could end up in love you could end up making love with your clothes off to someone with complications most of which, however, when they occur are usually apparent clinically as pain a tracheostomy and automatic respiration may be life saving I don't, I don't, I don't, I just don't understand my daughters. What happened? Tell me what happened?

The body turns beneath the light of the eye. I have held in the light of my eyes the bodies of those I have come to save. They are my people and I heal them. I am not afraid. I did not teach myself by operating on patients that have ten or twenty years to live. I would not do it. I would not risk their lives. I taught myself on those who were already condemned to death. Those who were already given up on. They came to me with their ragged bodies.

Recourse may be made to injections of fibrinogen if this can be made available by the blood bank even in the presence of a normal blood level this substance can be dramatically effective the patients soon learn to notice if the rate is not fast enough for them and give a good guide to those looking after them the prognosis is usually grave some patients show signs of cerebral depression immediately after operation once the temperature has reached thirty-four degrees centigrade the ice should be removed the patient can then be covered with a dry sheet great care must be taken to ensure that the temperature does not drop below thirty-three degrees centigrade because of the risk of ventricular fibrillation patients who regain consciousness at this temperature may complain of the cold the quicker the recovery after surface cooling the sooner it can be abandoned but if signs of cerebral depression return as the patient is rewarmed cooling should be reinstituted as soon as arrest occurs the cerebral circulation stops and unless it is restarted within three minutes at normal body temperature the patient will die of irreversible brain damage the diagnosis is based on the absence of carotid pulsation in an unconscious patient other signs may be present but should not be sought if in so doing treatment will be delayed "pinking up" of the ears and lips the situation is now under control return of a peripheral pulse and blood pressure and a rising level of consciousness of the patient all should stand by without moving the patient for at least thirty minutes IF THE HEART DOES NOT RESTART continue external cardiac massage placing the left thumb on the nipple in children and adult males ensures a cleaner incision and avoids subsequent disfigurement with adult females just move the breast out of the way the rate of massage is governed by the rate at which the heart refills IT IS USELESS TO SQUEEZE AN EMPTY HEART DAMN! Heart valves come in sizes, you have to choose the right size. It is important in the world to know the size of a thing. To look at a tube and think in centimeters. To ask for it and get it. To know what to do if the tube is wider than the valves on hand. To cuss out the nurses as necessary. To save life. To save. To observe for at least thirty minutes

IF CARDIAC ARREST RECURS TREAT IN THE SAME MANNER AS OFTEN AS NECESSARY if however the pupils remain widely dilated if ventricular fibrillation recurs on several occasions after it has been controlled and particularly if the fundamental cause of the cardiac arrest has not been eliminated permanent restoration of the circulation with survival of the patient is most unlikely.

I know the secrets, the heart secrets, I unweave the vessels and the heat and the flesh of the heart. I start with people who are already dead. I start with people who have a week to live, and I stand them up on their feet again, with the most perfect red rose within beating. When I touch them I feel the blood flow beneath the skin. I understand the desires of blood. I touch softly when I touch. Wherever I touch I feel the heartbeat through my fingers. I know what it is to yearn to live. Yearn to live my daughters. I have gathered them in my arms, I have known the strong ones to cry under my touch. They want me to save them and I save them. I know how they are made. When I place my hand upon them I know the dream of wholeness and health that is the imagination of the body. I have seen, within their bodies, everything going where it came there for. I have seen the purple blood turn bright red under my coaxing. I have called to the dead and said arise. I have ruled the kingdom of the dead and brought forth life by the light of morning. I love to operate in the early mornings,

I start with meditation, in hushed silence I think myself into the pounding mystery , I know every place where there is blood and when I will I call blood to myself. It is what I know. It is what I am best at. I play my fingers upon the pulse point and the watching souls swoon—my nurses, my secretaries, my assistants— I am chaste, I do not lie with anyone save my queen, Queen Camille. I long for no one else. I do not fall to lie with their bodies. I meditate in my office while waiting for the body to be prepared for me. I love the green coat and the run up the stairs and especially that brief winter cold that touches me when I run from the annex to the main operating rooms. I love to be ready when the buzzer calls. I love to know who it is that is calling for me. I love to understand what I must do to the lungs and the veins and the arteries and the heart of life when I am called. I have been called that they may be born again. Every person who has lain down upon my operating table has awakened again. I have come that the father who fainted in the way may now run down the lawns with his son. His own son.

Walk with me. Follow me. Come into the animal lab. Follow, follow me. My hand on the scalpel trembles the loins of they who watch, and they who turn away and those who rise from unconscious tables of blood into life, life. I know the heart and I love the quick red that fills it. With my hands warm upon the life clay—it breathes, lives at my command, my knowledge, my dream.

I can fix her, I can fix the dog up fine, perfect. I can take her heart out and I can put it back in again, she'll be barking tomorrow. You kids have got to understand this! Blood is power! You've got to look—look at her heart beating, she's beautiful, the heart! Look at her powerful heart—and my machine, it does the whole works. The whole works, right here! Heart Lungs Blood Oxygen—everything. Come and look at it. Look at me. It's ok. She'll live. Look at me. I'm right here.

You're not even paying attention, can't you hear what I'm talking about? The specific circumstance of the dog doesn't make any difference but I just want you to appreciate how important the body is. You keep thinking that spirit can live without body. But it's impossible. Spirit is part of the body and connected to it. I'm not talking about eliminating the spirit. I'm just saying that it lives right along with the body, closer than you realize.

This is serious. Look at this! See how I can do it? Cut her right out of her so you can see. Her heart. That's where it all is! That's not spirit! That's flesh! See, we put her in the basin with ice until I'm ready to sew her back in her again. Why don't you believe me? Why don't you ever believe? Her blood is still flowing without her heart and her heart is in the ice in the basin. Come over here and look at her, touch her and hold her. Yes, feel her, take her up in your hand. Isn't that wonderful?! Look at her trembling against your fingers and I swear to you tomorrow she'll be barking with that very heart inside her. Believe me, think about the body and believe in physical life, hold her heart in your hand without being afraid, feel the fibrillation, touch and believe.

So now give her back to me. Yeah, let me take her back so I can sew her back in her again...and where do you think your equal rights came from anyway? They came from the progress of medicine—much more than any progress of poetry! Do you want to know what enslaved you? It wasn't somebody's idea! It wasn't intentional male chauvinist pigism! It was massive pulmonary embolus, it was complications of coronary artery disease resulting in ventricular septal defects mitral insufficiency ventricular aneurysm and sudden death. It was stenosis of the paten arteriosus coarctation of the aorta vascular rings atrial septal defects tetralogy of Fallot it was transposition of the great vessels, tricuspid atresia aortic pulmonary window ruptured aneurysm of sinus valsalva it was illness of the body. It was misconfigurations of electrons and protons. Magnetic misattractions.

And do you want to know who freed you? Shall I let you know who freed you? *WE* freed you, damn it, we freed you! Medicine! Doctors! We gave you the life that none of your poets could give you. We gave your thoughts a chance! We gave people a chance! Do you think we could afford to let females read poetry or write it or go to school if we needed babies! If we needed babies because the population was being wiped out in childbirth and disease! Your freedom is a luxury I give you, medicine has given you the right to your own life, your own body—I came that you might have life and that you might have it more abundantly.

Watch the electric paddles. I place the paddles on either side of her, the heart, the dog's heart. She jerks as the electricity bolts through her, my hands stiffen for a moment and then relax as she takes over, the dog's heart, pumping, throbbing, beating, pumping, living, living again. My students are silent.

My daughters are silent. I look down at the pulsating life silently. Then I step away and my students close up the chest wall. This and this only is the Kingdom of Heaven. This is the multi-foliate rose you keep talking about in your poetry. The Heart.

# Atlantis

THE three brothers, Tommy and James and Chris, all sleep in a huge bed in the east bedroom. Saturday morning sunshine moves through the room, nodding on the rich orange bedcover, slanting against them. The bureau against one wall is heavy with thick ridged knobs, dark wood, and on top of it, dandelions in a glass, yellow heads drooping against wood. Chris moves his eyes around the room.

There is a picture of Jesus near the door, just above the light switch, a picture Chris has colored in the garish colors of Sunday School books, wide-faced happy children playing with sheep or looking into the face of Jesus or Joseph standing in his coat of many colors—but this is not a picture of children. Chris has pasted it on the wall. It is a picture of Jesus hanging on the cross with Mary and John weeping at the foot and at the bottom of the page it reads, "Mother, behold thy son."

The door is painted a pale blue color although the rest of the room is wallpapered in a delicate brown and beige fleur-de-lis. There is a toy box at the foot of the bed with a few storybooks on top. A yellow, mechanical dump truck is in the middle of the rug but everything else is put away. White curtains are in the open window and they move with soft puffs or are pulled slowly against the screen, there is an inviting woodland smell on the damp air. The light is so clear it seems later than it is, Chris is the only one awake in the house, and although

48

the dawn birds are still frantic, ecstatic, Chris lies on the cool sheets thinking it is already late.

Tommy on one end of the bed has twisted the covers into a roll beneath him. He is naked, having taken off his clothes during the night. His left hand grips the wad of sheet while the last three fingers of his right hand touch the wall lightly as he sleeps. He has been sucking his thumb and the skin has a wrinkled raw color. This morning he lies contorted, fiercely gripping with one hand and climbing the wall with the other. He has the lightest skin of his brothers, with straight, sandy-colored hair and a delicate face. He is the first-born son.

James is brown and happy and pure and other good things. Sleeping as he does between the others, he always has enough cover, he is always warm enough. He lies on his back, one arm thrown over his head, the other comfortably tucked under the warm orange blanket, entirely at his ease. His hair is kinky, his features round, and his lashes curl double against his cheek. Exhilaration. A contented rock between two volatile elements.

Chris looks around the room, his playful brown eyes dance up and down the sunlight that falls upon him as he lies beside the window. Sometimes he parts his lips in a smile and strums his fingers on the shirt of his powder blue pajamas. He has neither sheet nor other covers over him, for Tommy has pulled them all toward the other side and although Chris is chilly, he likes to smile and shudder in the sunlight. His skin seems to be as dark as James' but it has an uncanny quality. The surface skin is brown, but very transparent—so that a deep red color shows through. The intensity of the red changes with his moods so that although he seems very dark, he has a paleness that often blushes deeply. His hair grows in short dark curls that cannot be brushed smooth. There are birds and trees between him and the sun. He steps quietly on the floor trying not to disturb his brothers, today he is going away alone into the woods. Early in the week he had decided to do it. Since they wouldn't let him go to school with his brothers and he had to stay home watching them from the front porch, today he is going off without them before anyone wakes up. Even his parents are still asleep and the sun comes through the trees to the windowsill. He dresses himself neatly, as always, pulling each piece of clothing from its folded place in the drawer, holding the clean-smelling shirt to his face a moment, and then sitting on the floor he takes off his pajamas and puts on his corduroy pants and striped T-shirt, navy blue and white, his red tennis shoes, and carrying his red baseball cap he walks secretly to the door. No one there. He opens it slowly and then he is in the shadowy hallway that has no window to the outside.

He is afraid for only a moment when he sees the shape of his father warn away him from the far end of the hall where they have their bedroom, but it is nothing, no one is there, everyone is asleep. But then what is standing at the end of the hall? No matter. The house is asleep, no one knows that he is standing in the hallway ready to go out. And soon he is out, passing through the front room

49

and unlocking the front latch by standing on a chair, then he's on the porch blinking in the sunlight. He has already planned the way he is to go, the place is picked out, a place he had chosen on the way from church Sunday afternoon. Walking beside his father he had seen a clump of very dark trees, dark as the green of late summer, standing out over the tops of the other trees and bushes. There was a stream back there somewhere to the right of the road, somewhere beyond the curve where the meadow turns into bushes and then into woods. The curve had wavered in the sun as he walked beside his father, he had wanted to stop for a moment to see if it would stop wavering, but his father had been hurrying and anyway Chris didn't want his father to know he was interested in the place. Who knows, maybe his father even felt something strange there and hurried on past for a reason. Some secret is back there.

Chris steps into the road and waits a moment before following the way to the right. Bushes grow right up through the fences on both sides of the gate, the leaves are a vivid young green in the early Georgia summer. A rosy tint flushes over the pebbles in the road as the sun slants and sifts through the trees far down the field, down at the end of the farmyard that faces the road on the other side. Looped clouds touch starkly against the sky above the trees, looped extravagantly as loops of frosting on a wedding cake house. Summer smells of all the trees and flowers and bushes are sweet and airy, not yet thickened by day heat. To the left he doesn't know the way. No matter how often James takes him walking that way he always forgets whether there is a store or a town or other houses. But to the right he remembers, there is the church somewhere down there, but before he reaches the church there is the field, then the bushes, then the dark green trees.

He looks around him, up and straight ahead and to the left and behind; and then he walks off to the right. The way is long, longer than he thought. He walks close beside the hedges as long as they last but then there is only the dirt path with no houses for a while and the trees are back from the road. The path keeps on and he keeps walking. He has never been so alone. As he walks the sun comes clearly over the trees, far and on his left. On the right he can see the vague blue-black misty rim of low hills in the west. Soon the line of trees curves again toward the road on both sides and he is in a cool archway of trees.

This is near the place. On the other side of some sloping trees he finds the meadow, and leaving the road on the left, he walks toward a slight hill that is near his clump of special dark trees like an entrance. He struggles a little in the high grass, and his shoes are caked with mud, but he comes to the hill, there is a little stream on the other side—or maybe it is just a puddle of still waters, later he is never sure, and he sits down there to rest.

He is exhausted and has almost walked himself back to sleep—except the grass is too cool and the air also, forbidding, too new to trust, not warm enough to rest in. The grass moves here, the water is black at the foot of the hill filling up the dip between him and the place, where is it? Where is he going to find the trees? But he can't see them now as he looks around, stretching up, searching the tree crowns for the dark green he remembers. The leaves rustle into one another, the colors blur, he isn't tall enough, something is wrong, a mild ripple skirts the dark water, Is this the place? Maybe there is another field, and the archway, certainly the archway wasn't there before, maybe he has come too far—but then where is the church, or can it have been the other way? But here is the field and the bushes and the trees, but there are lots of places like that, lots of bushes and trees everywhere, and fields are always all over the place, there are lots of meadows, lots of green color—but why have the colors blurred so? And he huddles near the water holding his knees up to his chest. Waiting.

He is not surprised after a few moments to notice that someone is with him, an old vagabond sits just on the other side of the water, looking silently into the black water that holds no glance.

Chris looks at him carefully; his hands are dry brown and bony, and he rests on his right side, his arm stretches out against the ground, with his back to the morning sun. His shirt is a rainbow plaid that time has muddled and faded into quiet earth colors, browns touched off by scraps of melted reds, orange, yellow. He is too dusty for morning, out of place as he lies on the dew-heavy grass gazing into the water. His denim pants also have been worn into a dust brown color with no traces of blue remaining. He has been traveling in the dust so long. He has large skeleton feet and no shoes, the toenails are crusted brown-gray and the dusty color is so thick around his ankles that his brown skin seems flaked into white scabs.

His left hand is also against the grass and he doesn't move at all, his face is turned intently toward the water. And he is very intent, watching for something in the thick water. His unkempt hair is matted and tangled like dead underbrush after a flash flood has swamped a river bed. It even has dry twigs and caked mud cementing his hair and scalp in places. His face is a full healthy brown, freshly washed, and the eyebrows are thick and dark—his nose and lips are full also, full with blackness. Has he been there all the time? He is lying in the place where the water had been at first. The water had filled the entire area between the hill and the trees, but now there is a dry dirty place there on the other side, and tangled underbrush covers the entrance beneath the trees. Light is so strange in the morning, how can he sit there quietly so long? What was it anyway, that strange shape, not the one before him, but the other one, back in the hallway at home? What was the warning? It wasn't his father, it was too tall to be his father and there was nothing in the hall there, nothing at all.

How tall is he? Could he have been hiding in the house? Could he have followed him this long way? Chris hadn't watched the road behind him—so intent on getting to the place and now he can just about remember something pattering behind him, perhaps on the other side of the road, but so far behind that the shadow was dim as sunlight, dim in the sunlight, blending in with the gravel that sometimes moved in small wind gusts, an easy movement of air stooping and falling against the ground. How deep is the water? The sun is moving across the sky. What is he waiting for anyway?

Chris vaguely wants to go home but his eyes keep wandering from the bushes to the water and then up to scan the trees but it is hard to tell the colors and the old vagabond's face is blurred in the angle of the sun. And the grass is finally dry beneath him, warm and sleepy, but he holds his head up, blinking, remembering that he wants to go home and starting to move, but then he looks again for the dark green leaves that he had noticed on Sunday, those full fresh trees that had called him over the meadow almost a week ago. Called? Not in words, but he expected something, something more than a forest, perhaps an elf circle or something like that, or God. He just can't seem to stand up and go.

God was mad in the sermon that had excited him last Sunday. God was mad and had burnt up a city and only Lot and his daughters were left alive. Tommy and James had gone home as usual directly after Sunday School but Chris had stayed on with his father because he had read the title of the sermon. "John, Christ's beloved disciple." He had recognized part of his own name, John Christopher, in the words on the church bulletin board.

"I'm going to preach the word to you this morning. Do you love your Jesus? Do you love your Jesus? Do you love your Jesus? Yes, and Amen. I know you do, I know. But let me tell you something about love. You know there's more than one kind of love in my father's world, you all know there's more than one kind. And this morning we're talking about kinds of love. How do you love your Jesus? Yes I know you can answer me Amen, yes yes Lord, but how do you love your Jesus? Think about it.

"Now you all know, when the Bible was first written, it wasn't written in English, no, it was written in Hebrew and Aramaic and Greek and other foreign languages like that. And you remember how I went off to that Bible school, and while I was in the Bible school they taught me about Greek. Now I don't want you to think I'm going to stand up here and speak Greek, because I'm not. I'm not going to speak Greek but I just want to explain something to you and listen close, because you're going to learn something here this morning.

"You've heard the good sister read the text for today. You heard her tell about how the Lord asked Peter three times, 'Do you love me?' I know you've heard this story many and many a time but I bet you've never heard it explained before and that's what I'm going to do for you this morning. Now when this Bible, this passage right here was written back in Bible times, in Greek, well you know there were three words for love, not just one like we have, but three of them and they meant three totally different things altogether, yes Lord, these three words meant things so different from one another that if you all don't learn them right, then you never will understand what this text is saying. Now I don't want you all to think I'm going way overboard and this is getting too hard—you know I don't bring in extra things unless I'm sure it'll help, so just hold on with me while I show the text.

"Now the first word that means love means carnal love, you all know what I'm talking about, I'm talking about sex, I'm talking about lust after the body, I'm talking about those perverted sins for which the great God in Zion, Almighty Jehovah rained down fire and brimstone on those ancient cities of iniquity, Sodom and Gomorrah, leaving only Lot and his daughters alive. I say, you all know what I'm talking about. And the name of this kind of love in Greek is eros. Eros. Another name for eros is Cupid and I know all of you have heard of Cupid.

"Now the second word that means love means brotherly love, and you know what that kind of love is too. It's the kind of love between good friends, love between sisters and brothers. You go fishing over here with a buddy, helping and talking, the two of you just help each other as you go along, or it means lending a cup of sugar or a pan of potatoes, well, that's brotherly love, a good kind of love. And the name for this kind of love in Greek is philos. Philos. We have lots of words that come from philos and they all have something to do with this kind of love—Philadelphia means city of brotherly love, and so on.

"But brotherly love is not the highest kind of love. There's one higher than that, called divine love, divine love, godly love, and we could sit here all day before we figure out all the things it is. It's the kind of love that God has for every one of us, the kind that gave Jesus Christ the everliving son of the almighty God, to die for us on the cross. It's love that keeps on giving, love that can't help itself, love that keeps loving even if it never gets anything back, yes, it's the love of God, but people can have it too, John had it for Jesus and that's why he's called Jesus Christ's beloved disciple. And it's because of John's special love for Jesus Christ that John was the last of the disciples to die, and John got to see the holy city of the heavenly Jerusalem before he died and the end of all earthly things, the Apocalypse, was revealed to him when he was chained to the island of Patmos, yes, right there on the island of Patmos Jesus Christ himself came back for him. And the name of this kind of love in Greek is agape. Agape, divine love. How do you love your Jesus? That's what I've been asking you this morning, and now I'm going to go back and read the text using the right meanings so you'll know what I'm talking about. Here it is.

"'So when they had dined, Jesus saith to Simon Peter, Simon, son of Jonas, dost thou love me with divine love more than these others love me? Peter saith unto Jesus, O my Lord; thou knowest that I love thee with brotherly love. Jesus saith unto Peter, Feed my lambs.

"'Jesus saith to Peter again asking the second time, Simon, son of Jonas, lovest thou me with divine love? Peter saith unto Jesus, O my Lord; thou knowest that I love thee with brotherly love. Jesus saith unto Peter, Feed my sheep.

"'Then Jesus saith unto Peter the third time, Simon, son of Jonas, lovest thou me only with brotherly love? Peter was grieved because this third time Jesus said unto him, Lovest thou me only with brotherly love? And Peter said unto Jesus, Lord, thou knowest all things: thou knowest that I love thee only with brotherly love. Jesus saith unto him. Feed my sheep.

"'Verily, verily, I say unto thee, when thou wast young, thou girdest thyself, and walkedst whither thou wouldest: but when thou shalt be old, thou shalt stretch forth thy hands, and another shall gird thee, and carry thee whither thou wouldest not.

"'This spake he, signifying by what death he should glorify God. And when he had spoken this, he said unto him, Follow me.

"'Then Peter, turning about, seeth the disciple John, who loved Jesus with divine love, following; the same who had leaned on his breast at supper, and said, Lord, which is he that betrayeth thee?

"'Peter seeing him saith to Jesus, Lord, and what shall this one do?

"'Jesus saith unto Peter, if I will that John tarry till I come, what is that to thee, follow thou me.

"'Then went this saying abroad among the brethren that John should not die: yet Jesus said not unto Peter, John shall not die: but, I want John to wait for me until I come.'"

Tarry till Jesus comes for me is that what you're saying, really but I'm just a little boy and I don't understand all of that and I think I may be lost oh where are my brothers I don't know where I am I've been wandering around and around and how long is it before he comes back for me do I have to tarry forever and forever in church he said that I would never, never die but Jesus Christ will come back for me the son of God is coming back especially for me but I have to find an island of Pat but I'm afraid of the island I'm afraid, afraid, the field is so wide and I can't find my way oh where are Tommy and James oh where are my brothers, please please don't burn me up like those cities...

"Hey kid, are you ok?"

"Where are my brothers? Do you know where my brothers are?"

"Are you ok? Your brothers don't seem to be around here."

"Oh, I'm lost please don't chain me to an island. Please don't burn me, let me be saved like Lot and his daughters."

The old vagabond's white teeth grinned from his brown face. "I don't know, maybe you ought to burn up. You ain't nothin' but a little black boy, maybe you ought to die! What you got to give me if I let you stay here in Atlanta for a while, if I don't take you back with me to Savannah and take a stone and tie it around your neck and throw you in the ocean? What will you give me?"

"Give you? I don't have anything."

"You don't have anything...well, well, I tell you what, I'll wait until you're grown up and you think you're happy and I'll come and burn you up then."

"No, no, please don't burn me, I want to be saved from the fire like Lot was saved."

"Like Lot? You're sure?"

"Yes."

"You're a fool but ok, it's a deal. Meanwhile I'll show you down the road to your house."

"Ok."

"Do you know where you are now?"

"Oh, yes, I know where I am, the church is around that curve and this is the main road I'm going to run all the way, all the way, all the way home, home home, yes yes, run run run" but I was sick, he had put a sickness on me and my mother found me lost in the road lying there feverish with the chicken pox, chicken pox she found me, found me and carried me back home all broken out, he came to himself suddenly in the very midst of his winding storytelling path murmuring "let me die let me tarry no longer come now whoever you are to come to get me" murmuring "and who is this worrying me now, who the hell are you, I see you sitting over there staring at me, with your black face and your white eyes, Who the hell are you?"

"You never should have touched my mother." Johnnie's voice was the cling of chandelier prisms when a wind passes through and John Christopher shuddered upward and looked into her face. It was his last thought. "I have not three daughters, but four."

# Daddy

THE fourth daughter had come to her grandfatherfather finally escaping for her life in her seventeenth year running from Georgetown in the rain in the afternoon when Patricia her mother walked into the Potomac River, Johnnie, who was cast off by Diotima, Patricia's companion-lover who stayed a moment by the river before returning to México at last deserting Johnnie who finally escaping for her life that rainy afternoon ran from Georgetown to Washington to Logan Circle to her Aunt Eva where Eva through many days told the long story of the stone to Johnnie who then went to Turkey Thicket to the convent to her Aunt Sister Cynthia Jane who told the tale of the sisters to Johnnie and gave to Johnnie the letters of Patricia.

In the first letter Patricia wrote:

> Daddy,
>     I'm so angry with you and I feel broken and I don't want to move out of the house from the family all by myself I want to stay here with you. I've been throwing things around in my room but you didn't come, Daddy, I don't want anything bad but I feel so sad and lonely all the time and I never know what to do. I walked over into Rock Creek Park but it got cold and I started shaking. I wish you could like me more. Why won't you let me keep on living in the house with all of you? Why do I have to

56

move? I wish you could like me more. I don't understand anything.

patPat

and this was the letter on a ragged sheet of paper that had been torn from a spiral notebook the letter of the not having yet seduced each other, the letter of John Christopher getting Patricia out of the house into an apartment on Kalorama Road to remove temptation, the letter of Patricia having been forced to move away from the family by John Christopher.

Followed by the letter of the having seduced each other only once the words centered neatly on a sheet of blue paper:

Daddy I love you Pat your daughter

Followed by the long letter written in a small blue booklet with the words Howard University Examination Booklet printed on the front, the letter of the not having slept with each other twice, not yet, but wanting to, the letter of Pat having lived too long alone empty in that apartment on Kalorama Road, the letter of John Christopher trying hard, so hard not to go to her not to be with her not to want her not to think of her not to remember her not to desire her not to lust after Patricia writing Daddy, Daddydaddydaddy the letter of Johnnie not having been conceived Daddy:

Daddy,
I'm staying here in this place like you told me and I know I picked it but I'm getting scared of it the walls are too white and the maid you got me is always messing up my things I can't study at all and I keep thinking of you. I can't think of you anymore. This place is a prison. Sometimes I want to spread my books and papers out and study or close myself off in a quiet room and think—but there is no place. One table has all the stuff you left for me to do and the maid always wants the other table to set up my meals. If I set my books on her table, she places them in neat piles on the floor and I can't find anything. If I classify my books into areas of the room she conglomerates them into one—telling me I'm too messy. I can't find my books. I can't find any strength. And you haven't even sent over the rest of my books. Why do you have one whole table full of your things? I waited for you all day yesterday to ask you to clean it off but you didn't come over. I was going to dump everything off your table and tear up the work I had done for you. Then I would have put the table in the study and I would have had a

57

table for me. I would not have let you or the maid into the study. I would lock the door. But I can't dump your things on the floor because I love you, would it hurt your feelings if I dumped your things on the floor? Instead, I was so angry, I dumped my own things on the floor. My anger broke me in pieces. I threw things around and cried and cried. Then I went out trying to find my soul, O Daddy, they were my favorite things. I cracked the Venetian glass bird. I beat it against my suitcase several times. Your picture fell on the floor. It's still there, it's a sin for you to keep me in prison like this. Today when I left I went down to Dumbarton Oaks and I felt so happy and at peace coming back but I'm not, I'm scattered again. I live in a barren place. I know it's not your fault. I know you give a lot. I want a desk. I believe that if I don't find a way to read my books then I will go crazy. Whatever spirits there are punish me with insanity. I hate you, I hate your damn guts, I hate. Do I have to remind you that you promised to take care of me, and you're my father, I'm going to have to rebuild my life, I'm lost. You promised me that I would not be wasted if I tried to follow and be good and not try to sleep with you anymore. And I've been good almost two months now and you don't care and you don't even want to see me. Yesterday I spent the entire day in my study with no furniture and with nothing to do because there wasn't any way I could do anything and then you expect me to do your work too so depressing thinking about dying patients in this narrow empty place. Knowing how depressed I get you shouldn't place me in such confinement. I think you must be crazy too, you must be off balance to do these things to me and think you're doing good. Your own disintegrating psychological state keeps you from seeing what you are doing to me. I prayed this morning when I was in the garden, "Let thy beneficence enter my troubled spirit and give me peace." And peace came. I am not unaware of my value. I am sure there is some spirit who is fond of me. Today when my intellect had almost escaped me, surely something cleared the terror from my brain and I rose and walked a step and a step and a step. I wish I had a desk where nothing could come but my very own private reading and language things. And a room where I could go. You live in the full house on Sixteenth Street and you say you remember my barren rooms and walls. When I tell you I can't stand it you don't believe me. You tell me to decide what I want to do and you'll fill up this place but I'm afraid of myself and I don't know what to do. You don't

58

know how little I believe in me. You don't know my fragility. I beg and pray for sustenance. It does not come to me at all. And yet, today I escaped from you and this barren place. In Dumbarton Oaks I forgave you. I lay on the grass and blessed you because the fullness of the place overcame me and my soul rushed into this broken body and I smiled—I swear—I smiled. My first mistake was probably the biggest. I should have moved to Southwest where everything is happening instead of uptown. I am the one who chose this desert but it was because I wanted to be near you. I had no faith that you would visit me in Southwest and it is costing me my soul. No one can save my soul except me. I thought you could save me but when the clarity struck me today I remembered you cannot. When we decided I should move away from home, I said I would fix my study first. I knew what I needed. Instead of a desk I have bought perfumes, soaps, rugs, dishes. No wonder I am sad. And when night comes I read and read and fall asleep to dream of reading but wake in the mornings with the urge to vomit on the barren floors, these empty walls, these vacant windows. But I won't let me lose my mind. I will plant a garden here for all seasons. I will plant it alone if no one comes with me. I must do it myself. The burden is mine. My mind keeps slipping from me and I don't want to live. Why have I not perished? My greatest sorrow is the terror of some harrowing thought I feel called to know. My fear is that I am utterly lost in spite of being strong, powerful, and anointed. My fear is that these thoughts that visit me are not babblings.

Patricia

Johnnie read them as she left her Aunt Sister Cynthia Jane as she had left her Aunt Eva as she had left Georgetown as she was going now, finally, on a bus to Sixteenth and Kennedy streets, Northwest, as carrying a small suitcase she was going to knock on a door moving across Washington "Patricia my mother," the humming of the motor, the stops "my mothersister, Patricia" the sun pressing shadows through the heated pane, nod in the sun Johnnie, cozy, "My mothersister, Patricia, my auntsister, Eva" take the rosary bracelet from your arm, Johnnie, turn the large gold beads in your fingers half prayers ending in daydreams O peace, O holiness, "O my mothersister, Patricia, O my auntsister Eva, O my auntsisterSister Cynthia Jane, I am the fourth."

# Spring Mourning

CAMILLE. Bedcrumpled, hot, sweaty, wakes empty-hearted in early morning dark, fretting the empty bed. Sad, lost crying, a soft pretty lady nightloved, air licking gently her naked sweetflesh spread damp. Thighs open breath-pushed thrusting oh so smally the movement of her body undulates. A lovely lady but no lover to take what she quietly prepares for him waiting. Ooze soaks the sheet. No one else but alone. Camille wakes with her smell caught under the blanket, dawn, cut off, in the room high furniture angling from the walls, dawn, cut off, femalesmell oozing up through the shingles, skirting the edge of the chimney, stretching to reach the street, the sidewalk, the park, whimpering, cut off, caressing the lime green April leaves of the vagrant peering trees, cut off, sighing, amassing, smothering the house.

Camille has three daughters—Cynthia Jane and Patricia and Eva. Only Cynthia Jane is in the house, lying blank awake also in the early morning dark. It is a spring morning. But it is already too late. Everything is already lost.

Camille thinking. This is the coldest day of my life. I know it already. This is the coldest day of my life. This is the moment when I know I have lost love forever, this moment, this day, I know it, and that the excuses are lies. It isn't because he's overworked or because Patricia is bored or troubled or mentally ill. It isn't because he wants a son or because Patricia is confused. It isn't because he can't control himself or because he's a genius or because I failed him or because there isn't enough excitement in his life. It isn't because Patricia tries to seduce him or because she needs him or because his work calls him away so much or because I break his concentration and interrupt him. It isn't because he has special projects to finish and professional commitments to fulfill. It isn't because he doesn't have enough time for me. It's because I love him and he doesn't love me.

What has happened what can have happened did something happen before I slept last night? Camille. Cynthia Jane. Rain smell. Midnight and dawn, the turn of time, night ending and morning beginning.

Camille has three daughters.

Lately when John Christopher has risen at night to go to the hospital to see about the boy whose heart keeps stopping she has watched how softly he shuts the bathroom door behind him. She has listened to the brief pattering of the shower. He has left her without speaking. She thinks, he never did that before. She thinks, he does not want to talk to me. He doesn't want to talk to me and the patient he loves, the boy he loves is dying.

Last night he was out.

It should be dawn now. I'll have to get up. It must be misty outside. I've got to get up.

But I've forgotten, he wasn't at the hospital last night, it's already too late, he's out of town at that boy's funeral, the boy he loves. He's in San Juan.

Janie looks at the small wooden globe on her desk. They've gone out of town together. And where's Eva? Does she know, has she guessed?

Camille has three daughters.

Cynthia Jane is writing a poem. She struggles with the words on the page. She takes the letters of a word and spaces them out across the page. She makes designs and pictures with them she draws spirals on the loose ends and joins the loose ends to opposite sides of arrowheads, she builds pyramids on the arrowheads and swirling cones from the pyramids, and at the cone she draws a scoop of ice cream—but it's upside down. Her window faces west anyway—sunrise comes in dispersed. It makes the grass in Rock Creek Park green-yellow.

She wants to create something. Stuffed in her bureau beside neat piles of underwear and stockings are folders and notebooks of poems. Her first day at Howard University was the inspiration for one of them. She stood at the top of the hill that cuts through the city, the hill with Howard University on one end and Georgetown University on the other. She began a poem about beginnings, she imagined it when she looked at her city.

She saw how it lay before her from Kennedy Stadium westward toward the blue of the White House to the fog that rose out of the Potomac as it passed Georgetown. The bluewhite sky infected the landscape and in her suspension she imagined the branches of the river, the Anacostia and Potomac, she imagined them sludging toward each other narrowing toward each other in ridged triangle arms, pinpointing to the south at the Tidal Basin where the geometry is shattered and distracted by the circles and retreats of the Jefferson Memorial, Hains Point.

But before that. Before confluence speeds the slow rivers to the sea. Before that stands the Washington Monument. The monument with the pointed head as her mother says to the school buses she leads on tours of Washington land and water forms. The Washington Monument is pointed. The Lincoln Memorial is flat. The Jefferson Memorial is round. Marking the city.

Janie's poem is about that first day of college, because when she looked at the city, she knew she had found something big enough, something that needed what she could say about it. O lord what a beautiful city. And its Monument.

The Capitol has columns and ridges, it has decoration. The Jefferson and Lincoln memorials have statues, words are engraved, chiseled into their sides. Here a carved pageant, there a marble hallway, here the sky blazing between columns, but the Washington Monument has no faces, no columnar supports, no explanations branded into its sides. A shaft of blue-tinted marble from earth to heaven. No genial presidential face grinning cheery comfort across the city; no romantic portraits; no round or wispy additions muddling its corners—the obelisk is hard.

From Georgetown to Howard, the hill rests in liquid arms, Anacostia to the east, Potomac to the west.

The hill is a long hill. It rises from the Potomac in Georgetown, cuts across northwest Washington and at the edge of Howard it sinks into McMillan Reservoir. The poem is not ready yet, it still won't come.

Camille has three daughters. She is distracted this morning fiddling with the leaves of her gardenia, listening to Harden and Weaver on the radio, standing at the kitchen window in the early morning light moving around the house. The house is too big for me. The rug is white muffling my steps from the wide living room and the empty off-white walls—what time is it what day is it? She trips on the ledge coming from the greenhouse and almost sinks to her hands and knees. "It isn't anything, I'll be all right." Looking back at her gardenia plant.

Eva is last. She walks the streets like riotfire, she arouses them and keeps walking, keeps returning as if each return were pure and she a virgin, in the parks, in the slums, from Connecticut Avenue to Deanwood, she lies down in apartments, up against alley fences, or getting high in lesbian bars she...not think, no, not think. Cynthia Jane's poem has to be about the spiritual marriage between Christ and the City of God.

When Eva is frightened she sleeps with Cynthia Jane. On those nights Cynthia Jane holds Eva's hot body and wonders if she holds a changeling. Eva lays her sweaty face against Cynthia Jane's chest and grabs her around her shoulders, squeezing her fists into her shoulder blades. Eternal virgin. Eva. Renews her virginity with the moon. And maybe she is a virgin those times when I hold her through the night and how is it they never seem to know she's too young for that sort of thing they don't have mercy on her. Janie looks down at the page. She never gives up anything no matter how many she sleeps with. She escapes.

And Patricia. What does she keep trying to pull out of me? She is too passionate, I don't like the way she looks at me. Patricia. One morning I woke up and she was kissing me and I didn't like it, she had come back over from her apartment and was doing that, she wasn't even supposed to be in the house. I was angry. She never speaks of it when I'm awake, but asleep, kissing me like that. She must know that it is an evil thing to do, and me waking up to such kisses. Eva is an innocent child compared to that. Patricia is sick, she's incestuous. And now with Daddy. Patricia can't control herself.

At breakfast Camille looks at Cynthia Jane. Cynthia Jane looks at Camille. Each knows that the other knows that all is lost.

The telephone rings. The police found Eva left and lost and raped in the morning rain. And Chris is out of town at the boy's funeral. In San Juan. And Patricia? Camille and Cynthia Jane go in the car to the hospital to see Eva. "You know, Janie, Patricia took my nightgown."

Has he really gone with her? Has he gone—I don't have the strength to help Eva, I'm glad Janie is driving. I don't think I could drive. I think my heartbeat has slowed down or something. Maybe it's this drizzle making it hard to breathe, if I just lean back in the car seat, lean back here and open my mouth wide, I can rest my head against the headrest and I'll be ok. Where's my bag? Did I bring my bag? Oh, there, I'll just lean it against my foot, I'm glad I remembered to bring it. I'll just keep it right over here and then rest my head a minute, why is it so stuffy, the air is just staying here close to the ground, what's wrong with it? Why won't it move up and down? My soul is being winnowed, this is the threshing of my soul, I don't think Jesus prepared me for this, I really don't think it's fair. Am I a bad person? I try to help people and I go to church. I'm always volunteering to help out in the schools around here, I've got to do something now that this has happened because now I know that it's all true, and I can't just wait around for it to happen anymore because it's already happened. The air is too thick. But this seat rests my head what is wrong with the sky to make it bunch up like that so nothing can get through, I don't think it should do that, it should leave me alone so I can breathe, I'll never get through it like this, it keeps piling up everywhere with that sickening smell in it, it smells awful, like somebody who doesn't wash between the legs enough and the smell just piles up—what could cause that, it's putrid! What if it poisons me? And I have to keep breathing it anyway, nothing else can happen, nothing, this is the worst so I'll have that freedom at least when I see Eva, that the worst has happened and all I can do is keep on trying to do the best I can, because I am free now, I can act in freedom, now that I am in hell I am free. I'm covered with this murky air, why don't I fly up there now and see if I can get through, shouldn't I do that? but it makes me choke, this air, I don't really think it's friendly, maybe it would be better to stoop down where it's clearer, down over here, but I'd so much rather the sky were clear so that my lungs could really fill up strong it's awful, I can't breathe, why is the air pressing down on me so hard? who could have ever expected such a thing to happen, the very air? has someone dropped a bomb or something? what am I going to do? I think I can fly through it, I bet I could, if only I had a chance to try, I could tunnel a hole through to let sunlight back in, and I think it's about time to do that anyway, why should I have to live under skies like this? I shouldn't have to do it. Why don't I get out of here? Why don't I fly away through it right now, the trees and the mountains and the birds go up there and up there I could breathe not like down here, I just want to breathe a minute and then I'll come right back down, I will, I promise, and then I can go to see Eva with Janie it's hell down here, but up there everyone is free, from up there I can be an angel or a seraph, Janie is crying, she knows the truth, Janie is not supposed to cry because she has to take me to see Eva and I don't want her face all swollen, and if she would only stop the car a minute I could fly up and get some fresh air, and I could look down and find out what has happened since the beginning of time, I could see the Trojan War and the theft of Africans, and how they killed the Indians, I could see all the myths when they were born, and I could see all the way down here to the pit of hell, the annihilated, the deceived, the forsaken, the despicable, the wretched, injustice and sorrow and cruelty and despair and torture and lynching and murder and starvation and burning flesh and eyes put out and Eva raped I would see Eva raped and I would see my husband fucking our daughter, my husband fucking our daughter, my husband fucking our daughter.

# The Story Of The Stone

WILL you have a glass of wine, Johnnie? So Patricia and Diotima told you to do this? They told you to run to me from Georgetown if anything happened. And now something has happened—Patricia walked into the Potomac River and now here you are. Yes, I will tell you the story, as much as I know of it. I am glad you came to me. I will tell you about Washington as well. To me Washington is a stone, the particular stone upon which I was raped.

You've never even seen the Capitol grounds. It's hard to believe you could live so close to the main part of Washington for so long yet never come over here from Georgetown. Perhaps we should visit the Capitol grounds. The lawns and circles are a perfect garden there, precise, geometric. With clean flowers. The attendants must come at night secretly to wash and weed and polish the flowers unblemished red and green. I've never seen even one brown leaf there, they disappear during the night. And the colors of the flowers so clear and glistening you'd think they were enameled, truly polished. You have not yet seen Washington. It's the garden just to the north of the Capitol, looking toward Union Station, and it has a high fountain of colors changing patterns unrepeated in a night. You would like to see it? How strange it is to meet you at last, Johnnie. Rest when you need to, you ran from Georgetown to me as if you were running for your life. Seventeen years, your whole life, to stay hidden in Georgetown seventeen years. In all these years I never saw Patricia again. And now you have come running from Georgetown with my mother's eyes in your head. How you look at me. The fountain is of classical carved stone, marble as I remember it, a centered uplift of wet light dropping to fall over a smooth rim falling again to feed smaller fountains.

Fourteenth and U Streets Northwest is the crossroad intersection of the black community. In the Black Cultural Center there when I was young we talked about occult religions—African astrology, Egyptian magical ceremonies, we would be there in the corner of the Black Consciousness Reading Room throwing pennies for *I Ching* readings or using different lengths of spaghetti sticks to tell fortunes. We calculated the personality divisions of Yeats' lunar wheel. We made connections between European sorcery and central African tribal medicine. I had a crystal ball cut from a transparent green stone. I was the fortune-teller. In the evenings we sat wondering how the end of the world would come. Perhaps the sun will set yellow but green skirted, and the next morning it will rise in the west emerald green. Perhaps a black boy will be born in Harlem to raise the true black nation. No, I said, it will be a girl, and she won't be in Harlem, and she won't raise it, and the nation will not be true black. In a room on the northwest corner of Fourteenth and U Streets, Northwest. We stood in the streets staring at police there later when the city burned. There was always whispering somewhere in the building. Someone always high on something and someone always explaining freedom.

The Northeast center is Eighth and H Streets. I would go to the bars around there and prophesy black power coming. There were private parties. I could go in. I would whisper to someone at the front and go in to the party. They were always whispering behind chained wrought-iron gates, the rich artistic foreign service kind of blacks who grit their teeth and wouldn't move to a safer neighborhood, who kept saying how they just couldn't live if they weren't surrounded by blacks, who peered from behind steel bars and heavy chained fences. Lush low black souled furniture too modern for me to understand how to sit down. Somebody from somewhere always just back from behind the lines in Angola, Rhodesia, South Africa. There was always at least one coal black political activist who cursed me, cursed my high yellow skin as we stood appreciatively on the slate stone of the landlocked flowery patios. They would always be more worthy than I to be black, Johnnie. But you can't understand this, we had to show one another that we were really black, I mean they weren't nice to you if you talked too much about white things. They would always have given up everything for the sake of blackness, flaunting their dark bread and spring water sustenance at my pork devouring gut behind those high impenetrable police-protection wired walls that kept out the untrustworthy artifact-stealing rabble we had passed through trembling on the black streets to be together inside. We, the black intelligentsia, smooth, proclaiming our utter blackness in the galleries and patios of the parties where I was the fortune-teller, Johnnie, the prophet, making up their stories.

I lived in a hippie house near George Washington University where they always ate health food. I had to smuggle in the Kentucky Fried Chicken and McDonald's french fries, I wanted it, I was tired of tasteless rice, I wanted something to eat. Waking up in the mornings on a foam rubber pad on a board stretched over a flat sheet of stone stolen from the construction site across from the new library to keep above the roaches. I refused to live at home for a while. Walking the street. Washington, my inheritance. Washington Roulette. The street. Thug beating his wife in the middle of the street. With a stick. Beat the stick across her neck and shoulders until she fell down. Neighbors some laughing some quiet. Beat so hard. Just off Vermont Avenue near Metropolitan Baptist where I was walking by horrified. She screaming. He dragged her up from the street to beat her head against a car window. Bap. Bap. Bap. Her head flopping limp. Bap. Until I turned the corner where a car was pulled over to the side. Well-dressed neat black family inside. Father at the wheel. Daughter at front window. Son number one at far window in back. At near window in back, door open, madonna and child, son number two. His shorts dragged down to his ankles. His chocolate brown ass lifted above his head, on view to a gathering appreciative audience, the ass being loudly, resonantly ordered to still itself for the continued brutal application of the maternal hand, the ass being ordered to move itself only for the purpose of bringing itself into more violent and painful contact with the flailing hand that loved it, bruised it, shamed it, displayed it, spanked and spanked it, gave it an extra lick if it shied from a blow, two extra licks if it tried to ward off a blow with its hand, and beat it an extra minute to make it shut up its ungodly screaming, while the father waited softly holding the steering wheel waiting for the word to drive on. Washington.

I took a cab once to the National Gallery, walked around to the Smithsonian side and up to the east terrace, on my way to the statue of Mercury and the fountain, and passed a waxen- eyed poor white with his penis sticking out, leaning against the pink marble stone masturbating himself into the marigolds.

The wharf in southwest. I used to sit by the Washington Channel and eat cherry stone clams and crabs and clam chowder and oysters. I would eat until I was full. And at Neisner's before it closed up I would buy bags of peanuts in the shell. And they used to have the most beautiful goldfish and tropical fish. And plants covered the bottom floor it smelled like the botanical gardens. And I like the Folger Library with the windows gleaming the seven ages of life, transforming everything, always changing the outside gray drizzly sun. Have you been there yet? Will you have a glass of wine?

Lesbian bodies clutched together at Phase II in the middle of the night and I would never have a way to get home and I would always be so afraid. The male bodies clutched at Eagle's. There I stood back beside that special dark room where I was not allowed to go but anybody can look at the videos, or have a drink, or have dinner on the second floor, or visit the shop on the third. Vests.

Chains. They never sell those things in lesbian stores—just books and scarves a few postcards T-shirts—and maybe a key chain! In the afternoons on Saturdays I would have wine at DC Black Space after coming from openings at Lansburgh's Art Center. Or just go to look at the silver at Garfinckel's. Faces. I remember a lump of brown mud with apron behind the counter of the People's Drug Store just off Farragut Square. Her sunken blind mud stone eyes faced outward in the sagging brown cheeks with lips inaccessible to human expression, lumped up to take orders for bacon and eggs, inaccessible, lips that would spit at sunshine if sunshine should presume to touch upon the wall and in the square itself, Farragut Square, a wellkempt white youth, neat, clean, haircut, staring out from the concentric circles of his eyes, his hat held in front of him, à crayon on corrugated cardboard sign around his neck, swirled and twirled by the surging financialists, the sign reading, I AM HUNGRY. I am hungry.

I'm still not sure that I know what happened in our family. You'll have to go to the convent and talk to Cynthia Jane if you want to hear all of it. I just remember the rape, I lay so long on that awful stone that is still there, it's still there in the walkway beside the Old Carnegie Library. I remember the scene often.

I lay silently on the stone, Johnnie, naked, and so silently. He talked to me at first and I answered but then he was quiet and I was as silent as if I were his bride, I loved the silence, Johnnie, no one can believe this but I love the silence in which violence has no voice because the pain of that silence is stronger than the pain in my mind, the violence comes from outside of me and pierces me and hurts me so that for one moment I don't have to think my own thoughts. I imagined chains within the silence, to bind my wrists, to spread my ankles, I wanted to forget what I was thinking, desperately, passionately, I wanted to forget. It is because I wanted to forget. There is no limit. It is possible never to have done with knocking our heads over the same few biographical incidents that insist upon being the arbitrary markers of our lives. How many times? I have tried too many times to understand the things that tore our family apart. But there is nothing to understand, our foolish personal heads think there is something but there is nothing.

Only coffee? You won't have a glass of wine? It is foolish to go back, to expect to recover what we have lost in our lives. We can only go back obliquely and with filters upon our minds, we must decorate the horror of the past with the art of our present lives. We must make for ourselves a weeping wall, a stone barrier at the edge of clear vision, subverting it with carved panels of our moments of ascent and descent, we can stand upon such a wall and weep peacefully.

Let there be veils. Let there be protections and escapes from the knowledge we are condemned to work so hard at discovering. I'm glad you like the coffee. I get it at a shop down near Metro Center, across from Woodies. Good Brazilian beans with an Italian roast. And the shop itself is a pleasure. They have an old grinding stone and pounding tools on the shelves and huge burlap bags of beans lying all around. Whenever I go there I feel that I've walked into a nineteenth-century candy shop with a penny.

I have dismissed my mind, Johnnie, I have wanted not to know the meaning of what happened, and yet I would like for you to understand that this not knowing is a choice on my part, believe me that it is a choice, you probably will go to Janie in the convent. She can bear to see and tell the truth clearly and out loud. She will tell you things I will not tell you. I have longed for unconsciousness. I have had many lovers, Johnnie, and often they were not lovers at all. How much violence does it take to interrupt the mind so much that it cannot think? so that it can no longer follow in its usual ruts of pain? Yes, I will have a cup with you. It is an Italian set, molded in clay and hardened into stone, I like the gold flourishes, the deep green inside the cups, the spout. I think of the coffee beans as a form of gold, grains of gold.

At first we can trace the facts, identify all the forces and counterforces, and even assign blame, but it doesn't take long before the facts become lies, extensions of what we want and what we don't want to see, the facts are ourselves finally, and the more I focus on myself and the facts that mark out my life, the more pathetic I am, arbitrary in interpreting what happened, the mind is a stone running away with itself, a projectile incapable of perceiving the powers that propel it, it insists upon itself too much, it is hopelessly personal. The mind is incapable of fact.

I left Patricia to herself. I wanted to forget her. She asked me to watch with her while she died, to wait until death, loving. I was weary of her. I had enough to do to take care of myself. I guess I tried to be with her a little, but I just failed. Instead I have built this house in which to remember a stone. My lingering here is the memory of that anguish. I cannot forget. I loved my sister. I loved her but I couldn't concentrate on her for long.

She visited me in the hospital a few days after they had found me lying in the park beside the Old Carnegie Library. She asked me, "Will you watch with me while I die?" My sister. It rained the morning after I was raped. I lay naked on the stone. My clothes were matted up beside me. I will never forget Patricia's voice, "Will you watch with me while I die?" I told her I would be with her, and I thought I could hold her again. I remember holding her once in some autumn long before the rape, a small brown leaf caught on the window screen, cool air. "Will you watch with me while I die?" Such cool air.

I have no excuse. I left. I went to Europe. Patricia expected me to live with her. I agreed. But I left the country the winter you were born. Janie wrote to me that Patricia showed up in February with you and that Dad saw both of you at the Hilton. I missed everything. I only found out last year that you and Patricia were living in Georgetown. It was just last year that my mother told me that the two of you and Diotima were living in Georgetown without my father knowing, and that you had been mute until you were fourteen years old. In Georgetown. Just a stone throw away from me. So close. But back then I went away. I gave up. Do you know why you were mute for so many years?

Patricia believed that there was not enough room for her in the world. She thought the world was a good idea that had failed. She was appalled by all the missed chances for love and kindness everywhere, she would read the newspapers when she was in junior high school and she would focus on the most horrible stories over and over again, she would never cry, but she would sit in the gray chair in the living room and stare out of the window. Children looking on as lovers murdered mothers. Babies whipped to death. Ambulance drivers stealing money from the bodies of crash victims—but it isn't as if the stories were a surprise to her. They confirmed something she knew all the time. She would read of a crowded house that burned down because the people were burning oil in cans when the city turned off the heat, and her reaction was, "I thought so all the time, the world is not good." Horror and inhumanity validated her idea of life, a mythical belief that the world was damned. Apocalypse. By the time she was in high school she stopped reading newspapers and read only languages and literature, and she created myths. In her pregnancy she believed that you embodied the city's lost soul. Washington had lost its soul according to her and she would restore it through you, through her child.

I wanted to go to Europe so that I could think clearly because I too have many myths I believe in, and I had to figure out the difference between her beliefs and mine. Her myths hated the world so, and I think my myths are in love with the world, and I couldn't think. My father thought Patricia had left the city to have the baby, to have you, but I suspected she would not leave Washington so quickly and I found out that she was staying at a community center in Benning Heights. Diotima was doing volunteer work there. Patricia wrote to me the summer before you were born, just before I left for Europe. While I was away I stopped thinking about Patricia. I rested from thinking. My head seemed a cavern by the time I arrived in Italy, a stone abyss.

The train from London to Canterbury was cold. I thought I would not survive it. The windows cold, the seats the floor, cold. The only empty spot was near the end of a car where the door wouldn't shut and kept banging open at each rumble of wheels for cold air to hit me, rush me, cold blowing on me. Intoxicating cold, the car swayed I trembled the door crashed open cold air. I fell into a delirious sleep in which the crashing of the door back and forth, the shivering of my fingers knees lips in the cold rush, coincided with my breathing in and out.

I was feverish when I arrived in Canterbury, and I asked the taxi driver to take me to a hotel with heated rooms. He took me to a bed-and-breakfast place where I jumped under the covers without even taking off my clothes. I had pneumonia. I coughed and wheezed and ached the rest of that day and it wasn't until night, when the proprietor brought a heated brick wrapped in a towel and a pot of tea, that I realized the room wasn't heated at all. I had been too sick to notice. And I was too sick to move. I looked at the wallpaper. I measured how sick I was by trying to focus on the yellow parasols in the wallpaper. I was finally able to see the flowers painted on the parasols. And after a few days when I was better, the proprietor brought me a box of delicious cookies, and I sat and ate them while she fumbled around with the bed covers.

I went to Dover and left for Calais and Paris. I left Paris and went through Germany and Belgium and Luxembourg and the Netherlands, and up to Sweden and Norway by train. Stark cold. It was warm, warm on the train, but the land stark cold. Ice hills. Ungodly cold. In my mind. From Stockholm a sea of ice to Finland. I looked across.

A glimmer of light just at noon when I was on the train going still farther north, light aghast at itself, showing frozen cascades of fjords, white frozen light, still flourishes of water, still, and that is all of sun for a day, in Narvik, above the Arctic Circle in the dead of winter.

I stood in the icy street just in front of the Narvik train station. A street to my right led up a steep hill. If I could climb to the top of that hill I would see the sun. It was dark. It was two-thirty in the afternoon. I walked up, slipping and grasping at nothing, and came to the top. Perfect darkness. Black sky. The only light came from the ground, from the packed ice, the threatening mountains and cliffs and fjords and oceans of ice in the distance. I stood crying and the tears froze on my cheeks. "No, I will not watch with you while you die."

I could not give up myself enough to live with Patricia, and she wanted me to agree with her, to decide that nothing good could be salvaged from the world, that there was no such thing as life finally, there was only task, a good or evil task. There was no such thing as playing or peace. I could not live such a life. I would die, she would use me and I would die. She didn't know how to care about my way and I could not give myself up to her. Sometimes she melted when I held her, when she wanted to rest with me, but where would she go while she was resting? She would not stay. She seemed not to be with me. So cold. She walked within the images she constructed in her mind and she never felt me touching her. She did not care for me finally, she needed me and used me. As if my touch were a way of distracting herself from her soullessness. Or was her need for me a mask blurring her desire for someone she really loved? I gave up. Patricia was the Arctic Circle on the twenty-first of December. I cannot bear such cold. I came down from Narvik running like a maniac. It was St. Lucia's Day, the day the sun turns in the sky and comes back. All the children in the streets held candles that touched and altered the buildings and walkways, they were singing, calling back the light, but the light didn't answer fast enough. I left to find it myself. I did not get a hotel room. I lived in the waiting room until the time for my connection. When I came into Copenhagen I was losing my mind altogether. I saw Patricia's body in the landscape, a glacier, and me a pathetic little flame huddling beside her trying to keep her warm. Why couldn't she have loved the world? Why couldn't she decide to live? Why couldn't she enjoy it? I bought a ticket for the sun and fell down to Genoa.

Genoa was warm. I was worried that I would freeze there too—there was snow and a thick milky fog as we came down through the Apennines, all the farmlands were white, but the sun came out just before Genoa and it was lovely on the ancient buildings, yellow plaster and classic marble and huge blocks of warm gray rock surrounded by green hills with large villas facing the bay. From my hotel I could look down on the street market—I had delicious lunches there. I was really happy in Genoa, I didn't know I could be so happy. Walking on the warm beach, the air was a little cool on the streets away from the sea, but the beach was warm. I played in the sand, watching the conversations of old people on the benches, the young families who came during siestas, Papa, Mamma, and the children. It felt like the beginning of time.

I remember sitting in an open park surrounded by a half circle of tall arches covered by thick vines along the top. I cried again there because a grip loosened from my heart. The ice melted away in Genoa. How I wanted for us to be together all in love with one another. I wanted the whole family to stand in a circle in love with one another completely and forever. I wanted us not to be afraid to touch one another all the time or any time we longed for love or comfort or rest or even awakening, Johnnie, I wanted us all to be forever delighted with how happy it was to be with one another, and to be free to hold one another in sleep. But it all turned into something else for us, and they would not let me be free to love them and touch them. But where does sisterhood end? They said it was not sisterhood but seduction. They said they never would have thought of lovemaking if I had not touched them. They said they knew that my touch was innocent but theirs was not innocent. That I awakened them and they became not innocent. They told me. I just wanted us to be together in love always.

I did not want the family to be separated. I was too late. First Patricia moved away into an apartment on Kalorama Road and then Janie was deciding to become a nun and I was alone. On the days when I stayed home I would get up in the morning and watch my mother pruning in the greenhouse, playing with the flowers, picking out the grass from between the stone edging and the roots of the rose bushes. Dad was spending longer and longer hours at the hospital then, and Janie almost never came home from visiting the convent house near Catholic University, and Pat was losing her mind half the time in that empty apartment where I wasn't supposed to go. Dad got an apartment for her before everything got really bad, and a maid—one of the patients he had cured. But our house there on Sixteenth Street was so still and lonely. If it hadn't been for our own maid working her way through the house, I wouldn't have been able to tell one hour from the next. I began to rest from these scenes when I was in Genoa. I wrote

Dad from Genoa and asked if he would give me enough money for me to stay awhile. He agreed.

You say she did not drown in the Potomac, that she is not dead, that you saw her singing and dancing above Three Sisters Island with Janie and me before you saw her riding above the river, that you saw her raise her arms to the city of Washington, that you saw her lift her right hand and step out above the water as if into a chariot, that she did not drown, that she spread out and dissolved southeastward into the horizon just above the water, that Potomac came and got her, that it was Potomac who carried her on the top of the river, above, and that is the sweet low chariot upon which she left you, that your mother Patricia deserted you, that you don't want to be without her. It is a vision. Light touches the river. Diotima sees Patricia drop like a stone, carried away by the current. You see your mother fly home.

I dropped out of high school and wandered the streets of Washington. My mother told the school she was educating me at home but all I was doing was walking the streets depressed. Sometimes I didn't go home at night. I just walked the streets. The walk ended at that stone.

*I am the stone. They have walked away from Carnegie and gone over to Martin Luther King having left me leading to these empty library walls, empty reading rooms at the end of marble stairways.*

I turned toward the hippie, "How dry I am!" but I wasn't drunk. "Oh, I'm sorry." "Think nothing of it." "That is, I mean, I thought you were having trouble or—I don't know. I just thought that maybe—well, did you fall?" "Falling I can handle. It's this goddam bush that's in my way." "Oh, well, I..." "C'mon, c'mon it's a joke, baby, laugh!" "I'm sorry, I didn't understand..." "Nobody asked you to understand. I told you to laugh. Now, laugh!" "Well I can't just..." "Fuh-git it."

*I am the stone. They have walked away from Carnegie and gone over to Martin Luther King having left me leading to these empty library walls, empty reading rooms at the end of marble stairways. I sit here at Seventh and K across from Hahn's Shoe Store—it too will be forsaken—and stare up at midnight.*

I lie there in a side room on the third floor of a lesbian commune, falling. I have bought several pounds of bananas and the stench of them hangs in the hall. I lie undisturbed, voices touch and rattle somewhere beneath and sometimes a step penetrates the hall. I lie there falling toward the bottom of my mind. Voices crack somewhere beneath but think of a mat squeezed into a corner with me upon it feeling the spaces in my head utter quietly my body, my body curved, lumped, hustled, leaning against the wall, the blanket heaped ragged, my dirty bare yellow feet straggling the floor, I breathe the air in and push it out again, breathe the air inward quietly, unfocusing my vision sleepless eyes, lifting my hand to the curtain, lift it, a cloth cloud against the wall, I watch speckles break into molecules, sleepless wakelessness, undisturbable, utterly concentrated.

*I am the stone. They have walked away from Carnegie and gone over to Martin Luther King having left me leading to these empty library walls, empty reading rooms at the end of marble stairways. I sit here at Seventh and K across from Hahn's Shoe Store—it too will be forsaken—and stare up at midnight. When they first learned to read I was the one who led them toward the chapters of their desire.*

I am defined between perpendicular and horizontal I am a soft lady lying on a mat I am sinking how I sink. Often space congeals around me I accept the air and push it back again sweat beads my neck is slippery with it my hands awkwardly clutched around a rumple of curtain but think of a mat in a room pushed against a wall where old psychedelic posters are disintegrating and plaster is disintegrating and the floor has a gray rug so old so walked on that the surface has woolly curds that roll like dirt from a wet ankle after an insufficient bath.

*I am the stone. They have walked away from Carnegie and gone over to Martin Luther King having left me leading to these empty library walls, empty reading rooms at the end of marble stairways. I sit here at Seventh and K across from Hahn's Shoe Store—it too will be forsaken—and stare up at midnight. When they first learned to read I was the one who led them toward the chapters of their desire. They are faithless.*

I am not asleep my grimy curls dip under my chin as I lie on one side, the curls of my brown silk hair twisting beneath my neck and held against my breast with a nail. My right stretched-out arm under my head, slightly my back touches the wall I face the door.

*I am the stone. They have walked away from Carnegie and gone over to Martin Luther King having left me leading to these empty library walls, empty reading rooms at the end of marble stairways. I sit here at Seventh and K across from Hahn's Shoe Store—it too will be forsaken—and stare up at midnight. When they first learned to read I was the one who led them toward the chapters of their desire. They are faithless. They have not kept their promise when they promised they would not forget me. No. Now they go to Ninth and G where they worship their new god.*

"Why did you let yourself come to this?"

"What?"

"Why did you let yourself come to this? And holding a gun."

"You don't know me."

*And others go to Founder's Library, the Moorland-Spingarn Room at Howard University.*

"No. I've never seen you before."

"Why aren't you afraid? I can kill you, I've shot people before."

*And others have even set sail for the Library of Alexandria.*

"I believe you."

"Why aren't you afraid?"

*They wore me down to this fragment of myself and then they left me.*

"Afraid? Yes, I should be afraid. Yesterday I would have been afraid but today there is an angel watching over me lest I should dash my foot against a stone. If only you could make me afraid, how good that would be—if only you knew how—tonight—you see my father has gone to San Juan, one of his patients died you see, a little boy, a cute little boy—you see he's gone to the funeral—you understand—and if you only knew—but you can be my angel and watch over me, a scraggly white angel with blind blue eyes. How ugly you are."

*So many passions passed over me. So many passions stepped on me and walked away.*

"You're crazy. You're a crazy high-yellow nigger."

*I thought something else would happen. I didn't know I would lie alone through this April night. I had thought that something would happen on this night.*

"Ugly white angel with blind blue eyes, grizzly faced, broken toothed, sneer lipped, tell me then, what do you want of me?"

"I want to strip you naked and give your yellow pussy a hard fuck."

"Put down the gun."

Down.

"You're very dirty." Her unhappy brown eyes look into his blind blue eyes.

His grimy hand on her stockings, fumbling at the waistband. "Have you ever raped anyone before?"

"Yes." Pressing her against the side of the Old Carnegie Library he got his fingers inside her waistband of her underwear and stockings and he pulled them down to her ankles. She looks at his sickly white scalp, his straight hair sticking up. He has recently wet it somewhere. Did he stick his head in a fountain? As he stands up again he lifts her skirt with his hands, holding it around her waist trying to look at her.

"Drop your skirt off." It drops as he scrapes her blouse open with his fingernails. It is too dark to see her well but he begins to make a humming sound in his throat as he stares toward her breasts. She watches him.

"Unfasten me." A violent white angel. His blind blue eyes glancing, blinking. She waits for him to beat her into the stone and mutilate her. "Unfasten me and open your legs."

He has no underwear. Even before she unzips him he is bulging against her hand. She drops the pants around his hips. He is pleased. He smiles at her. A sincere white angel smile. He holds her against the library wall by her waist, then pulls her slowly to sit on the stone, the cold shudders her, the cold reminds her that something is wrong. ("Something?") She tries to remember. As she sits he pushes open her legs, her knees wide apart, her stockings stretched, ugly, he quickly turns her to lie on her back on the stone and ripping her underwear and

75

stockings away from her feet he sticks his dirty penis in her. The knobby stone bruises her and it is cold. ("Pat. Where is Pat?")

*But the stars have lied to me, and the new grass that gnaws at me has no memory and the rains have washed away the night leaving me only this naked prophet, yellow-skinned and sleeping, plump and lovely, newly raped and fallen.*

# The First Time

PATRICIA sleeps and dreams that her father rises as a moon, his deep brown body touched with red, a blushing brown, rises as a moon touched with cloud blurred with a day's rain, the softness of his body presses upon the room. She reaches for his fingers through empty air toward no one.

It is in San Juan when she shows up at the hotel. He sends her to a separate room but she won't stay there. She won't go away and when he goes to take a bath they are there taking a bath together. She is happy then. At first she sits on the bed listening to the running water, wondering how he looks. And outside it rains. The orange and black curtains are closed against the dampness but the dampness comes through. The sound of rain washes through the room.

It is a lonely sound beyond the warm rush of her heartbeat. Her body fills with the thought of him, her head droops, she is tender, vacant, preoccupied, sitting on one corner of the bed wondering if he will let her sleep with him. She has followed him so far and has never slept with him before. And there is a chill in the room. She stands up to turn on the heat but then stops, she stands listening to the bath water running.

"He's in there now on the other side of the door and I'm here listening to the sound of water and I wish I were there with him. How I love the look when he looks at me and he tries to look away from me and I fill with heat but he won't touch me and I cry for him but he won't touch me and inside I ache because I want him and I don't know what to do and I didn't know I could want him so

77

much. I wonder what he looks like. I want to look at him. I want to go to bed with him. It is cold. The bathroom door is shut. He doesn't want me to come in."

And as the slashes and whips of rain strike the window she undresses herself, unfastening the sleeves, the sash of her dress, looking toward the closed door of the bathroom to see if he will look out at her, but the door remains closed. Her stockings, her slip, she lays them down. The soft white underthings, she takes them off until she is completely undressed and still the door is closed. Then she takes out a nightgown, a pale blue nightgown with a pale blue satin bow at the neck, but she does not put it on. Instead she goes to the closed door, and bashfully she opens it, and looks around at him. He does not speak. With her head down she walks softly there and steps into the water, and kneels there in the water between his legs before him.

She cannot lift her head. A few drops of water have scattered over her body, over her breasts and the space between them, the full drops ease down and as they move they catch the light. She clasps her hands together on her knees. The movement of the water shifts the light. And he only has to look at her to see her.

He looks at her head, her thick fuzzy hair, completely entwined, a perfect brown circle except for a slight leftward turn. She holds herself slightly off center. It is this that troubles him so. He cannot withstand this; to see her there kneeling, lost, in love; her chaste body exposed, innocent and entirely lovely, her subdued breathing, and below her breasts, the muscles taut and expectant. He looks at her. His eyes travel gently against her body beneath the water. He sees that she is very beautiful—yet he is still free until he looks again at the brown halo above her face, her face diverted away from him, this slight turn touches his deepest thought and sweetens between his thighs and she sees the slow rising motion of his sex and she reaches for him, he raises his hips toward her gentle pulling, and when the tip lifts above the water she bows in one smooth motion and kisses him there.

Quietly, lost, he turns her around and she leans her back against his chest. She feels his hardness against her and pushes herself close. With one arm he holds her against him, easily encircling her so that her left arm is held tightly against her body. Her right arm is free and floats unconsciously in the water. Her head leans against the brown arm that holds her. He buries his face in her hair and then, after swishing the soap in the water he gently bathes her, soaping her body under her chin, her shoulders, touching her nakedness, pulling sweetly at the rose chocolate tips of her breasts, he lingers there leaving white bubbles of soap melting into the beige-white crevice and down toward the water.

And his hand also moves downward, caressing her abdomen with the soap, moving in a shallow circular motion, around and around, up to the base of her breasts, distorting them for a moment with the pressure of his fingers, then down to where his other arm grasps her, slanting from her waist on one side over to her hip on the other, he moves the soap over her body, and he feels the lovesickness of her body under his hand, he feels the shuddering under his hand, and quickly, uncovering her with his arm, he pulls her tightly against him, and pressing his fingers between her thighs—untangling her hair, he touches her and eases his fingers around and up into her body.

She rises up out of the water. Slowly, easily. Arching her back, shuddering her head upward, twisting her neck, turning, her fingers outstretched and trembling in the water, her hips circling and rising to meet his hand, and his fingers playing within her, and his thumb pressing against her, he feels the throbs as passion fills and empties, it kisses and falters against his hand.

She doesn't know what to do with the feeling, she whimpers, not knowing if she should cry, and she feels like crying, clings to him grabbing his shoulders as she twists her hips away from his grasp, yet his fingers follow and she cannot get away, writhing in the water she cannot get away, and he won't let her go though she turns and then she does start to cry because she is afraid and she cannot get away and her fingernails scar his shoulders but he won't let go.

He turns her. He stands and lifts her from the water and carries her to the bed. He places her so she can receive him but she turns away, hiding under the pillow. But he takes the pillows away and turns her again on her back and this time she lies there looking up frightened at him, yet she lies there, open, her arms above her head, the back of her hands against the headboard, her legs also open but not as he has placed her, she pulls her knees closer together, but he holds her from closing her legs, not entering, not even caressing, but almost protecting, hiding her from his own eyes, as if he were remembering a sin in looking at her there. Then he plays her body, all of her, her legs and her stomach and her arms, he feels for the warm places, her ears, knees and suddenly the first kiss full in her mouth, their damp bodies close upon each other, and she has never expected this. She has not imagined that something could happen. She struggles to push him away, kicks and twists from under him wrestling his arms from around her body, she turns him away from her and she means it. He knows that she intends truly to push him away and he doesn't fight for her but lies surprised on his back with her holding his shoulders away from her. And she almost rejects him entirely right then except she oddly changes her mind as a strangeness begins its slow circles within her and she opens herself above him, suddenly panting as she moves her leg over him, kneeling above him, she grasps him in her hand and sits upon him, squeezing and massaging him with her tightness, pulling him into herself, with warm liquid oozing down upon him, dripping down his thigh.

Pain holds her away from him for a while but she eases herself down, then the slow riding begins, raising her hips and then down, rotating her hips away and then closing deep around him, lifting herself each time more slowly more deeply down against him and lifting her arms high above her, high into the air in an arc above them, then down to play with him, pulling the black curly hair that tangles in hers as they come together, she fingers the top of his skin, chest, arms and face and then up again, her head and her arms above him, "Butterfly" he names her as she lifts above him, and circles and down. He holds her hips so tightly she lifts him from the bed each time she rises. And her circle of passion sweeps out in a circle to the edge of her body, every pore opens for the conclusion, it comes to her edges, her knees, her ankles, she twists into the final heat but especially her hands, explodes from the center to culminate in the fingertips of her right hand which she lifts alone into the air and she looks down upon her father and calls him, "Daddy, Daddy!" He sees the flush rise in her as the moment comes, and she begins to fall, and quickly he turns her beneath him, pushing into her and holding himself there, and then he is no longer her god, nor her king, nor her lover, nor her father, but he is an erected penis urging itself into a female hole, only that, he is a penis with a female hole to enter, and does enter it, expending itself himself within live female flesh, pushing and pushing and pushing in, without will or hope, only a risen penis inside a live female. It expends itself, John Christopher's penis in Patricia his daughter, with climax swirling outward from the center, turning and turning, passion and possession sweeping them out and away gyring, widening as liquids mingle between their legs, they are swept into silence. Caught in that sensual music, caught, the golden bird, caught by a touch, Patricia, prettyPat, patPat, patPat, whispering possessed in her forgotten baby voice as her father sleeps, "I don't like you, stop hurting me, don't you hurt me any more, you're mean to me, if you hurt me any more I'm going to kill you when I grow up, what are you doing to me Daddy, that hurts me, is it a fire Daddy? it hurts me, did your finger put a fire on me Daddy?" Shaking and trembling and no one to hold her as she shakes and trembles in her first orgasm, not this time but the first time, the first time, hidden, forgotten, violated by a touch of her father's fingers upon her two-year-old clitoris, "is it a fire you put on me Daddy, I don't like you Daddy, you're mean to me Daddy, don't hurt me anymore Daddy, Daddy my hands and my feet don't feel good, what did you put on me Daddy, I hate you Daddy, please hold me, Daddy I'm scared lying here shaking and trembling, I hate you Daddy please hold me, I hate you Daddy please hold me, I hate you Daddy please hold me, I hate you Daddy please hold me, please hold me, please stop my hands and my feet from trembling, please calm the fire you touched onto me, Daddy, Daddy, Daddy, please hold me Daddy I hate you, please hold me Daddy, please love me Daddy, please touch me Daddy, Daddy, Daddy, Daddy, stop hurting me Daddy, don't touch me anymore, I hate you, I love you, please hold me Daddy, Daddy, Daddy, I hate you Daddy, I love you. I love you. Daddy, Daddy, Daddy, I love you." Whispering the words she had no words for in the beginning, during the first time, as he sleeps fifteen years later her body stiffens into a catatonic X of horror, violation violently enforced pleasure and pain, she whispers possessed by the words she did not have at the beginning, "Daddy, Daddy, Daddy. I hate you, I love you, I hate you, I love you, I hate you, I love you, I love you, I love you, Daddy, Daddy, Daddy."

# Chalice

AND Patricia whispers to Eva, "Will you watch with me while I die?"
Eva wakes it is dawn they have found her
Eva wakes she is in the police car
Eva wakes they are doctors they are feeling her pulse
Eva wakes they are walking her to her bed
Once a sister asks a sister, "Will you watch with me while I die?"
"Patricia?"
It rained last night after the filthy rapist touched her. Her white yellow body is caught in the twists of sheet, in the black blanket and white sheets—the black blanket swaddling her pale body.
Once a sister asks a sister, "Will you..."
Between the clank of the cart and the lifted hand holding the medicine, Thorazine, desolation.
"Eva was taken to the psychiatric ward today."
"What a time for Chris to be away in San Juan."
"Let's drink coffee with donuts."
"Let's discuss baseball."
"What do you think Chris is doing in San Juan?"
"Let's do anything."
"Her senses are gone."
"At least she isn't in pain."

"Where is Patricia?"

"She didn't know us in the hospital."

"I wonder if they'll catch him."

"Why didn't Patricia get over to see her?"

"I ate a grilled cheese sandwich and my stomach won't calm down."

"Maybe Patricia isn't in town either. Maybe Chris and Patricia are out of town."

"I drank a beer real fast."

"This is awful."

"I slept."

Sleep.

"Will you watch with me while I die?"

Eva lies sleeping in the hospital. And Patricia whispers to Eva, "Will you watch with me while I die?"

If you can't see, sleep.

"Have a cup."

"No."

"Have a cup."

"I don't want to wake up. Don't wake me up."

"Have a cup. It will sleep you deeper."

On the ward it is gentle because finally a nurse brings something orange in a cup. Thorazine. God of thunder and lightning. I wake up to take it and suck at the white paper cup. The taste is sweet on my tongue but the aftertaste is bitter. The nurse is in white and the sheets are white and I am a soft pale yellow against the sheets. And the nurse is down the row and I lie waiting for sleep. It comes quickly, and I balance against the green ceiling, falling and remembering upward, forward in time. Patricia chases John Christopher. John Christopher chases Patricia. His Finger and Penis form a high glorious X in the sky. Thunder and Thorazine and Rain.

On the ward it is gentle. When I walk in someone screams out, "Here comes another one." I drop my head—crazy—I wonder if I'm finally crazy. Is it possible? "They call me Candy." She grins at me. She plays a loud radio. She is a snake with thin sneaking legs. A snake with legs. Her legs too thin. Her body ripples. The breasts are too small. A snake with small breasts. "What they git you for?" My head drops down. I am soft. I look up from beneath faint eyebrows. My eyes are beautiful. The nurse pulls me, "Come on, dear." Crazy.

The nurse has a white dress and white stockings, and white shoes but her face is black. Black nurse in a white dress. She is a sweet lover undressing me. Her hands play softly on my body. I want to die. Her hands take everything from me gently. When they found me this morning I was raving but it didn't hurt.

"You may have everything." And I give it to her. "You may have everything." She fastens my white robe in the back. I am embarrassed. Then I sit

83

on the bed with my pale legs hanging down. My legs rusty and poor-looking, my heel cludding against the metal of the bed, bars to hold me in. I don't mind. I want to stay here forever. I want to fall asleep. "What is your name?"

"Why are you here?"

I clasp myself, clutching at my body, is this how I'm supposed to act, is this how to be crazy? "I won't tell you." Clutching my body, fighting away sanity.

"Well, I'll tell you, I'm here because of my nigger. Almost everybody in here is here because some nigger done messed them up. I lost my nigger and ain't been right since. I'm a alcoholic. When they brought me in I was screaming."

"Who could have messed up so many of us?"

"How come you're here?"

"What's your name?"

"What was that?"

"I ain't talkin' 'bout jes one!"

"This chick acks crazy."

"What's your name?"

"You talk funny, are you from Washington?"

"Thou hast said so."

"What?"

"Wuz you born here?"

"Yes, right in this hospital. I was born on Ward Twelve."

"But now you're on Ward One."

"The ward for crazy people."

"Yeah, it's jes like them kid songs, ten little, nine little, eight little Indians..."

"It's niggers, seven little niggers."

"Naw, that's John Brown John Brown had a little nigger chile."

"I was born on Ward Twelve."

"What?"

"What's your name?"

"There are twelve gates to the city."

"What? Washington?"

"Did she say she was born in Washington? She don't talk like it."

"Yeah, an' she look half-white anyhow."

"She's probably educated."

"You go to school?"

"Twelve gates."

"What the fuck is the matter with you?"

"What's your name?"

"What are you here for?"

"I want to die."

"Goddam! Really?"

"Yes."

"Shit! Ain't nothin' worth that. What? You in love with some nigger?"

"No."

"You some funny colored chile."

"Where'd they pick you up at?"

"Ladies, will you please go back to your own areas and leave the new patient alone?"

"I'm jes talkin' to her. Can't I jes talk!?"

"Miss Snowdon needs to rest." Miss Snowdon is bundled up sleeping in a white robe. All of god's chillen got one.

Wake up. Wake up to sleep. They mix it up like Kool-Aid and pass it out in beakers. A black face in white handing me a white cup with orange liquid. A black nurse with white shoes walking the ward from one sleep-sodden femalehead to another. Sleep.

I wake to a black hand reaching orange liquid toward me. "Oh, may I?" And there. At the last bed on the left side of the ward, the dispenser in her nightly round, between the window and the catatonic. Among the suicidal elite, there she stops.

"Do you want some medicine?"

"For me?"

Orange liquid in a white cup in a black hand.

"Nurse?"

"Yes?"

"Nurse?"

"What is it you want?"

"Is this for me?"

"Yes, this cup is for you."

"Will you watch"

Once a sister

"Patricia?"

"Eva, will you watch with me while I die?"

Who is fighting? Who is fighting? I only asked for rest. I lay my head upon a stone to rest, I want sleep, let me sleep. I don't want to see. I don't want to look up at the stairway to heaven in the midst of a desert. I don't want to go upstairs into that room. I don't want to wake on holy ground. I don't want to wrestle with the angel. I want to sleep. Let me sleep. Who is fighting? Who is doing battle? Is it god who does battle, or is it sleep? Let me sleep. Where are you taking me? Is it the end of the world? I don't want to go. I want to stay here and sleep. Let this cup pass from me, this vial, chalice, grail, urn, skull, let it pass.

Sleep.

*And the eagle who stands in the sun flies down to Sixteenth and Kennedy Streets, Northwest, in Washington City and into the window of the Snowdon family home and sits in the wall of the room where Eva lies. And Eva hears a great voice out of the wall saying to the seven angels, Go your ways, and pour out the vials of the wrath of god upon the earth.*

Eva lies there content. It is a beautiful day.

*And Diotima poured out her vial upon the earth.*

Eva lies quietly on her bed at home and she is not confused, cuddled in purple and red with her peaceful eyes awake or asleep, her fingers clasped under the blanket, it is hard to move, the air is too thick, the sweet honey air framing her pretty curls on a satin pillow. Eva did not want to come home from the hospital. She is tired, very very tired. Her face is soft. Her visitors are surprised by her round eyes. Eva is no longer at home in her mind. She sighs. She dreams farther away.

*And Eva poured out her vial on the sea.*

And in the afternoon Cynthia Jane hesitates before entering the room because Cynthia Jane is afraid to talk to Eva but it may be that Eva shall never be afraid again.

*And Cynthia Jane poured out her vial upon the rivers and fountains of waters.*

"Janie?" Cynthia Jane grips the knob of the door, her dark chocolate brown arms are tensed, her eyes are afraid, there is fear in the folds of her skirt, she turns her head toward Eva in fear. Their eyes meet and Cynthia Jane runs to Eva for comfort, she lays her head in the blankets, cries for a while and it's Cynthia Jane's wet face in Eva's lap, Eva's unclasped hand pulling and caressing Cynthia Jane's dark wavy hair.

*And John Christopher poured out his vial upon the sun.*

Day colors almost dry around them yet the purple glows darker, stranger as evening comes on. The purple seeps into the woodwork, shades the walls—only Janie's skin seems darker than the purple, only her sad face lying restfully on Eva's purple bedspread. Light disperses outward, more soft ray after ray slowly leaving, murmuring in the rose curtain, rippling the silk rose curtains with a kiss, a light kiss fluffing through the pale color and day transparencies dimming out around two sisters. Eva looks down on her sleeping sister. What can it be that makes sunset come to the city so brokenhearted? Why is it so hard even in the softness of these pillows, in the velvetsilk bedroom, even from here the city is dying into a greater dark, the beautiful city. Are they anxious tonight? Are the black children still playing in Anacostia and Clifton Terrace happily their loud games or have they softened into crying, or are they silent this evening looking out at the sunset? Are they riding bikes and playing jump rope? Are they happy tonight as from East Capitol Street to Clifton Hill they see the Washington Monument blink its red eyes, north and east? Do they think something has happened? Has something happened?

*And Camille poured out her vial upon the seat of the beast.*

" Eva?" It is the eagle of the wall leaning toward her in the dark. "Eva?" "Yes?" "Are you ready to leave?" "Yes."

*And Patricia poured out her vial upon the great river Euphrates.*

Looking up at the wall, Eva sees a plain of sand and upon the sand a very black female child dancing or playing in the golden light. She walks out of the sun and she steps quickly over the sand. She is a very black female child bouncing across the sand. The lonely voice of god comes back from the wall. "Eva, who is this black female child?" "She is the awakener." Evening comes darkly but the golden light floods the wall where the black female child sleeps on the sand.

On one side of her a white male sits and stares into the north but the golden light reaches even to him and after it pierces him he stands and turns toward the place where the black female child sleeps. Likewise on one side of her a black male sits and stares into the south but the golden light reaches even to him and after it pierces him he stands and turns toward the place where the black female child sleeps. "Eva, who are these nations?" "They are Africa and Europe. They come contending so closely that they fall as one nation into sleep upon the River Potomac. They shall awaken."

Now a crowd of teenagers are scrambling in a field, the light returns. The young ones are laughing a made-up game digging up the soft ground, singing folk songs,

"Swing low, sweet sweet chariot, coming for to bundle us home" when one of them, a very black female child, uncovers a pointed object, a carved stone, which the groups tries unsuccessfully to lift from under the sand. "Eva?" the god calls out, "Eva, tell me what place this is. Tell me what the children have found."

*And Johnnie, a very black female child, poured out her vial into the air, and there came a great voice out of the temple of heaven, from the throne, saying, It is done.*

"It is a stone, the stumbling block, the beautiful smooth white piercing stone upon which my city has fallen, it is the Washington Monument that, in fulfillment of the dreams of the people, shall stand forever, covered under a field of sand." "Truly, Eva?" "Truly." "Will it be covered so deeply?" "I cannot see so far."

"Hey! Hey! Wake up you two." Patricia is smiling and Cynthia Jane and Eva start back from the happy figure in the doorway as if she were a vision.

# Another Faerie Tale

ONCE upon a time there were a king and queen and they had three daughters. And the first was Cynthia Jane, and it was she who was the poet. And her skin was black, and her eyes were deep brown, and her black hair was thick waving around her head and down. And the last was Eva, and it was she who was the prophet. And her skin was dusky white tinged with yellow, and her eyes were light chestnut brown, and her hair was silky, sandy, curly and long. But the middle one was Patricia, and she was called patPat, and she was the beloved child of the kingdom, the singer of wise songs, the knower of all speech and the languages of all peoples, the one they had all waited for, the pet, the prize of the age.

And the name of the king was John Christopher. And King John Christopher had an enemy, a great adversary, who had been prepared for him at the foundation of the earth and that great adversary had followed him out of the seas and marshes of the south to destroy him. And the enemy, that great adversary, came into the kingdom and found King John Christopher upon a throne of gold, with Camille, his queen, upon a throne of gold, and between them in three golden cradles were Cynthia Jane and Patricia and Eva. And the enemy, that great adversary, saw that Patricia was the beloved child of the kingdom, the one they all had waited for, the pet, the prize of the age. So the enemy, that great adversary , said to himself in his heart, "This child is the one thing, the one most favored by John Christopher, she is the prize ordained for me from the beginning, from

88

before the time Europe strode and Africa strove together across the Atlantic Ocean, glutting the sunken lands with blood, Atlantis, Atlanta, confirmed to me at last by John Christopher. I will steal the soul of this child and the kingdom will fall." And so the enemy, that great adversary, came before the throne, and casting dust into the king's eyes he carried away the soul of Patricia. And Queen Camille cried out for the soul of her child. And Cynthia Jane cried out, "If the soul of Patricia is not returned then I am the poet of the end." And Eva cried out, "I can see the end and the soul of Patricia will never return and I am the prophet of the end." And King John Christopher never heard them because all he could hear was Patricia singing her story of wisdom from the cradle and he fondled her for the sake of her song until she changed her song, which became one small voice whispering "Daddy," and it was Patricia calling for him, and he caressed his child and lifted her in his arms, and kissed her soft skin, and wept over her beauty and touched her where he should not have touched her and loved her more than was well.

And life went on and the kingdom throve and Patricia lived on without a soul. But the time came when it was hard to live without a soul so Patricia prayed to god to give her a soul. And god said, "A child you have within you and she is your soul come back to you." And Patricia lay upon the flood plain of the great city where she was delivered of her child and that Childe is me, and she called me then Kristen Dolores, meaning "she before whom Christ sorrowed," that is to say, Johnnie. And god said to Patricia, "Your moment is ended. Before this birth all the ages of your people have longed for you, but from the moment the child is born, thereafter Johnnie is the soul of your nation." And so it was I was born once upon a time.

D.C. General Hospital. The puffed white pillows were pushed to the upper right corner where the bed slanted upward, the pad under her was soaked in blood, she was crumpled toward the foot of the bed, her neck uncomfortable against the bend in the mattress. It was a hard birth. The nurses had no time to wash her afterwards, she had asked for a drink of water before she fell asleep— but they would not give her a drink of water, it had taken three doctors to get it all out of her, she slept with a clear saline liquid dripping into her arm, one drop at a time. She dreamed of a drink of water.

And the baby was the marvel of the nursery. The baby with polished black skin, they had never seen such a color, not just brown, but really black, entirely black, a tar baby warm and fat, looking out on the world with clear white-blue eyes. A marvel. And the mother lay paled out and drained, lay against the white sheets, her sandy-brown skin, dry, her thin fingers clutched the sheet. There had been so much pain.

It had begun in the middle of a thick dreamless sleep in her room at the community center in Benning Heights. The fever had dropped and she had been able to fall asleep in her room. There was no one with her—she lay on the bed trying to relax as the strange motion in her belly pulled and pulled—yet it was not exactly pain. It was thinking a new kind of thought, a felt thought. The wrenching within her, the pulling asunder, it was not really pain, it was an orgasm that could not release itself. She counted, one (pause) two (pause) three (pause) and on and on each time it began and the whirling fury within her—but no, it was precise directed motion, it did not waste itself, it did not spread, it intensified within its parenthesis eighteen (pause) nineteen (pause) it was not so bad, it was like falling outward toward the end of the world, it was like twisting the universe into an arrow and shooting it through the heart of god, like being god before there was anything, and dreaming of something, and speaking the word, and then for it to begin, the abdomen heaving, weeping, expanding, to have creation kick up its baby heels and clear out, diving headfirst away and away forty-eight (pause) forty-nine (pause) fifty (pause) it was like staring at a miracle, it was something her mind could not believe, her eyes widened and took in the patterns on the ceiling. Wind images shuddered the white curtains, the embroidered vases had an orange glow even in the dark omylord—but she did not cry out, she just did not believe it.

But by the time she counted to sixty-five it would stop, she could feel the tide recede around her muscles, the tension in her belly would turn away, easing down, and each time she turned to the telephone to call the hospital, somebody, but she had no strength to call home, twenty miles, twenty-one, twenty-two, twenty-three, (pause) twenty-four five six (pause) and before she could reach for the phone she was asleep. Then the muscles would remember, turn and come quickly back, and she would wake to count again. Sometimes it was hard not to cry. She twisted from side to side and held herself. But even when she clasped her arms over her swollen body, when she thought for a moment and wished that god would have mercy, i wish i wish, she did not really say anything, she only counted and rolled her body from side to side. And she became so overheated. And she wanted her mother more than anything twenty-six twenty-seven twenty-eight miles from home and then again, sleep.

But then she woke and her time had come with its horror. All the other contractions had fallen away after she reached sixty. She could not believe it. She was not frightened until she reached a hundred, it did not stop. It swelled. It grew. It expanded straight up. She prayed to her god then, whispering to herself as she kept the count. When she reached two hundred she almost decided to give up, to tear the sheets, to scrape the paper from the walls, to bounce her head against the windowpanes—anything to release her body from that stretching pull, that wrenching away—but she did not give up, she lay there and rolled from side to side.

But there was no mercy. When she reached two hundred and fifty her voice faltered, her tongue, she could not take any more, her mind broke, her thought broke, it was too much. So she stood up. She turned on the light. She walked to the window. And her fibers were slowly rending. Splitting from the base of her belly upward, and all the tender things that were there, tearing, ripping, the raw skin spurting blood through the aching pores, the jagged plump petals of flesh puckering outward like an unfolding rose. She kneeled and started again to pray but her mind was too broken for prayer and she wanted her mother lord I'm only twenty-nine miles from my home will they not come for me? But there was no stopping it. She crawled to the bathroom and hung on the rim of the seat trying to throw up. But she could not throw up. There was no escape from it. There was nothing else. There was only this unfolding horror, the coming of this child.

And at the last it was more like death than anything. She could not move. She could not have moved for Gabriel. It was the end. Squatting there in the bathroom, it was the pitch, the top, there could be no more. And lo and behold it was suddenly over, the baby was crying on the bath mat and Pat nauseated above it.

And in the reprieve she managed to scoop the baby into the mat and crawl to the phone and they came and got her, resting the child between her legs, the cord still strung between them, and the quick breaths of the baby seeming loud as they rode through the snowy streets. It was only two blocks to the hospital, they just had to cross the Anacostia River on East Capitol Street, two blocks filled with a white silence, silence and Johnnie's breath. There was no stopping the bleeding, her womb would not give up the useless pulpy flesh but poured it out, all the doors opened, every drop rushed to the center, flung down the tubes, the heart pushed and pushed trying to empty itself, patPat, patPat, and it almost did. They changed the sheets so the doctor could see. She looked at the nurse and said, "It hurts so much," but then she just lay her head down. They had to keep her awake, she kept trying to die. ("In the name of Jesus Christ of Nazareth, might I have a drink of water?") she thought.

The nurse mumbled something in the corner, pulling out cotton, gauze, anything, but the womb belched out its liquid, fouling the instruments, clotting on the trembling hands—yes, trembling. He called for another doctor, he did not know what to do. And he cut deeper and deeper within her, trying to get it all out. She felt the nervous punching instruments circling within her, now pressure against her stomach, now her spine, and the pain was a bright glistening thing, it swirled her in its mysterious colors, pale tangerine, lime, magenta mixed with white, an unmerciful pain sinking its sharpened teeth oh so sweet and slowly through her swollen abdomen, yes, glistening with pain. ("Water") Even in so short a time it seemed her skin began to wither, her hands, the thin fingers transparent, her skin forming minute white lines, the lines of the flesh exposing themselves as patterns of wrinkles. And they could not find the right kind of blood anywhere. And her own blood in a riot, the veins, the arteries emptying onto the sheet, every capillary lifted its stops and barriers, her heart was trying to give its blood away. ("Water")

91

And the brain, or whatever it is that lives in the brain, whoever it is, she wandered within her skull, muttering to herself, If, she gasped and cried, she lay like a dead thing, If thou hadst known who it was who asked of thee, she was looking for him but she could not find him anywhere, where was he? where? beloved, why weepest thou, they have taken him away, beloved why, away, thou shouldst have asked and I would have given thee living water ("Water") "Please, may I just have a drink of water?" "No, you cannot." "Just a finger of water on my lips?" "It would make you sicker." ("Just the sound of water, just a sprinkle of water on my head, just a faerie tale about water") "PLEASE, in the name of Jesus Christ of Nazareth, might I have a drink of water?" And they had to change nurses because the one they had could not stand anymore.

And finally the third doctor came in green clothes and a pale green hat, and before he pushed the knife into her she sat up for a moment, and she reached for his hand and she held his hand for a moment, and as she held his hand for a moment she looked into his face, and after she looked into his face she took her eyes away, she took her eyes and her hand away and she lay back down, and she closed her eyes. He was quick and precise. She felt the tug in her belly and then it was over except for the vomiting. She emptied her stomach into the pan. The taste was bitter. "May I have some water?" and then she fell asleep.

She dreamed of a drink of water. ("For whosoever...what was it?") But they gave her no water.

# Forsaken

FOGGY Bottom. My earliest memory is mist, thin fingers of cloud straggling down the Potomac, stepping as pale lovely ghosts, wisping into scattering blossoms, flowers chilled to the bone; then hanging quietly through the gray air cold, cold, the wandering smell of wetness, the cold in my boots, my hands, and running to catch up with Diotima, down the path through the puddles, reaching out for her, Diotima, Diotima, wait for me!

The towpath. I suck in the cold air so deep by the spattery rocks, the splashing against the icy rocks where Diotima walks, leaving me behind close to brown-dead grass and thornbush filled with icicles and the brown twigs glittering so pretty I walk in with them, crunching and breaking the silvery blades to stand under one of the larger bushes, enchanted with the overcast sky above layers of twinkling thorns. I am enclosed by the thornbush until my body fills, until cold is what I am and by breathing deeply I inhale a glittery lining inside me like the ice on the thorns, I want to be shiny like that. Shiny and pretty and gentle because thorns are gentle to touch when the ice smoothes the points.

But she stands there, Diotima, on the rocks so long, climbing up and down looking over toward the Potomac, sometimes moving so fast or looking down again at the gravel—I think she has lost something and run from under the bush down to the canal shore to the grimy area where the dampness leaves a sticky black edge; it is like glue and when my heel squishes into it and I feel the cold with clumps of gravel and dirt molded to my boots and Diotima looks up suddenly, "Go back," and I am so cold.

Fantastic graywhite forms float into one another, reform themselves in massive puffs that hang near my head, or whip through the air, white streamers to hold. And across the river and downward I see those strange buildings glimmering so sad in the fog, Rosslyn, on bright days I see them from my bedroom window, but we only walk down by the canal on cold foggy days, or when it is almost dark. I like to go out walking.

Diotima seldom takes me out in spring and summer. I look down on the Whitehurst Freeway and see the cars passing, and light sparkles on the car windows and on the canal and on the river. At midday I have to blink to look out at everything. Diotima tells me that my room is at the top of the house so that I can see far without trees in the way. But I'm sad, and Diotima sets up a playroom for me downstairs on the second floor and I sit with my toys near the back window and look across the hall to where my mother sits at her window on the front.

At the farther end of the playroom Diotima places a red enameled writing box, which opens out to a gold felt writing surface—or perhaps it is velvet. I want to have it—although I don't know how to write—it is a writing box from China. And along one end there is a place for ink and brushes. It is inlaid with minute designs all in shades and tints of red. From a distance it seems all one color unless direct light strikes flat against it, and then a single lily or a flock of crested birds dance out of the wood, or a forest of shimmering pine trees. Once in midsummer when a stark slant of light comes through the back window, a group of figures float across the lid and into the room...they are such gentle people. I walk toward them holding my new wooden train. I remember the fresh wooden smell of my toy, and the hardness of the wood in my hand and the slow walk, which flittered the light on the top of the writing box, and how they greeted me. China is good. China and Japan and Indonesia and all those places. And standing among the figures and swaying I look up beyond the white rug of my playroom to the other side of the hall, toward my mother sitting in a lavender dress looking out of the north window.

But late autumn and winter are the best times because then Diotima takes me outside even in the day and we walk up the towpath until we come to that rocky hill where the river turns from the northwest and I play on the rocks all day and look at the river. There is one big yellow rock there that is my very own rock. My mother's favorite place, down near Key Bridge, toward Three Sisters Island, is ugly, reddish brown, covered with thick undergrowth that rots and stinks in the autumn and in winter freezes to an impossible tangle. There is no brush on my rock, and northward along the river, as far as I can see, there are lovely river castles that the Potomac sculpts from the piled rocks, like homes I could live in all the way up to where Diotima says they turn into mountains. But the time for wandering far up the river is short, winter is short in Georgetown.

Sometimes, during the evenings of the warmer days, Diotima takes me out walking with her. There are always many, many people on the street when we walk out, and some of them even have skin color that is black like mine, but we never talk to them. There are many stores and they sell things from all over the world. Diotima tells me you can buy anything you can ever want right here in Georgetown. You don't ever have to leave. We have brick sidewalks in Georgetown and Diotima says brick sidewalks are nice. Diotima says I shouldn't ever want to go on the other side of Key Bridge to those tall buildings called Rosslyn. And I shouldn't ever want to go on the other side of P Street Bridge, where there's a big city. Diotima says it's even bigger than Rosslyn. But they don't have brick sidewalks over there. I don't want to go there, Diotima tells me, I don't want to go there. She tells me, I would rather walk up to Dumbarton Oaks, or down to the Tea and Coffee Shoppe or over to Georgetown University. And I don't want anyone else ever to talk to me.

Some people are talking about Diotima while we sit in the café at night. "That's not her child, the child's too black, I bet she's the maid, some nigger is trying to show off by having a white maid. It's a shame." Diotima and I bring ice cream home for my mother. When Diotima goes in to buy the ice cream I stand by the door and look at the children. I think they are nice children. It is a long, long time before Diotima tells me that the big city next to Georgetown is called Washington, and that it is the capital city of a very powerful nation.

I never go to school and they don't find out that I can read until I am fourteen. Diotima reads stories to me and I learn to read that way but I don't let them know. I learn because I overhear my mother telling Diotima that I'm retarded and my feelings are hurt. My mother often says things like that. When I am seven she tells Diotima that I am retarded because of my father, she says that is why I can't talk but she doesn't explain it. After that I often walk down by the Potomac and wonder who my father is and why he has made me retarded. This is the beginning of knowing for sure that I have a father who is a person. Diotima tells stories in which people grow out of the sand or air and I think my father is like that. I know Diotima has a Spanish father from down south somewhere in México, even my mother has a father on the other side of Rock Creek Park who is a heart surgeon at Howard University and who sends me toys from "Grandfather." I know all this from listening to their conversations and I think I should have a father too. But before I overhear them I never think my father is a person—that is a surprise and I walk along the towpath wondering about it.

I suppose this is my first discontent because the games I play by the water become empty after that. I choose corroded chips of pebbles and with colored rocks, twigs and gravel I arrange my own village. The elongated pebbles, curved like bones on the ends, I stick in the sand for trees, cementing hills of stones and mud and I use the sticks for houses. I spend hours marking smooth roads in the gravel with flat pieces of wood. Paths lead from puddles through the village to the hill with a special little footpath leading to a waterfall that I make using canal water and a paper cup with holes punched into it. The water spatters irregularly down the hill but after much molding I redirect it to the stream bed that leads to the large pool of water. When all this is working I push small black pebbles along the road as people, placing groups of people in front of the sticks that are their home. I keep the extra black pebbles I collect at the bottom of the large pool of water so they are washed clean when I need them, black and shining.

But this game is empty after I think of my father as a person. Why have I never heard of him, where is he, and most of all, does he know about me? I feel forsaken, as if I can know more than two people in my life except I'm retarded and it's my father's fault and where is he? "Where is he? Where is he?" I ask myself hundreds of times, walking up the Potomac to the rocks where I stand with the cold sun on my head thinking how it is more peaceful for me when the river and gravel are my father.

But even this anguish lulls after a while and it is only in strange times that I remember my father. Most often these times come in the night—once I dream myself into a state of terror and wake in the darkness of my room—I lie there imagining that snow has been packed against the four walls of my room, which is a burial mound, and I have been left here to die. I am just a fleck of heat and light struggling and turning around against darkening white walls. Even as I try to focus in the dark, the space around me narrows and in the bottom of my chest there is a fuzziness that holds me back from breathing, that makes me want to cough but I am too weak to cough, too weak and too still to hunch my shoulders and cough. Mold, it is mold seeping into my snow cavern and unraveling the coverlets, mold floating on the air and sinking into my breath, twining my ribs and spinning cobwebs from my flesh, holding me in an ache that sinks my bones into the bed. Then there is no wall but only ice arching over a bed of packed snow, ice crumbling by its own heaped pressure, falling over me, dislocating into chunks—ice canyons exposing treacherous layers as they float above me massive and unconscious as the undersides of icebergs shattering lazily above the wreckage of ships—there they lay, those ships with their lost people, at the bottom of the sea, just as I lie sucking the air that choked me. But I don't choke, I rest waiting to die, waiting for the heavy ice to crush me into the snow of that oceanic darkness and the shadow of that sea is so dark that blood and ice are the same color beneath it—which is the color of my black body, I wait for my life to die.

But suddenly I change my mind about dying, I throw off my coverlets and standing in the middle of my bed, remembering that I have a father, I shout, "Daddy, Daddy!" and wake up the house. Oddly, it is my mother who comes to me then, bringing a strong, pure light. She takes me from the bed and down into

96

her room while Diotima only looks in through the door astonished. I have never spoken any words out loud before in front of them. They don't know that I can talk. It is my mother at last wrapping me in blankets, sitting me over by the heat, and kissing me yes, her kisses on my forehead, my cheek as I shiver under the blanket. I cry so long, so much then—she holds me softly yet I keep crying with loud sobs. And as the night passes over me and I sit there shivering and crying, nothing can warm my body. Even when my mother drapes herself around me, her arms stretching around my blankets and comforters. I feel no warmth. Diotima fixes hot chocolate for me but I don't drink it and then she leaves my mother and me entirely alone and goes back to her room.

Then the night stretches out long and quiet. Although the room is filled with light, dark images still appear to dance against the walls. I see maroon specks of flickering spots with clusters of lines reaching out from them, spiders dancing between the walls, but whenever I try to focus they are gone and there are only empty circles floating against the wall; circles where there is no wall, and seemingly no air, yet I'm sure the spiders are there. My mother's head is against my back but I know she is not asleep. And the night stretches and stretches, overstaying itself above our huddled room, holding the sun below the horizon with the toes of its black feet. I am cold. Pale cold blue wolf creatures creep from the pores of my mother's arm, the arm presses against me, holding me to her. I see them step out of their small caverns and shake out their hair in the light of the room. Wispy as pale blue smoke, they hold one another's arms and running in a circle, stir up a wind, I shiver. I am so cold it seems I am within the circle, and the center of the circle is ice. Then realizing that I am in the circle of my mother's arms, I feel an Arctic whirlpool dashing around me, swirling. But I withstand it all the night, cold. My mother waits until she sees I do not give in— it is a challenge and she thinks I'll run away, she thinks I'll run to Diotima—but I endure her cold. I am cold but I am not afraid. I know I don't want to die. I know no matter how close her ice caverns come to crushing me, I won't die. And I discover where the cold sleeps, I find its source in my mother—and all other cold on earth is only an intimation of the cold she has in her, yes all the cold of the world from all those plains and mountains that pull ice and sleet out of and over the sea is only an indication that my mother has somehow passed through the land, she has passed through and scattered the powder blue lavender of cold, she has packed houses and people in pale blue cold and flung the north wind against the earth from which it shatters into heaven to reach us here in Georgetown. I am not afraid.

Finally she sits up and moves around in front of me. After a few moments she slowly speaks to me for the first time about her desire. "Johnnie, will you go to find him? Your father? If I cannot go will you go? He must come to me. He has to come. You know that. You called him tonight so you must know. My life will extend into yours. We'll be the same person and you can bring him back.

Will you go? When the time comes, will you bring him? He will come to me again, Johnnie, little girl, there is a curse also on you." We are staring into each other's eyes as she says this, I look far into her dark brown eyes. "Who is my father?" but she doesn't answer me. She is shivering. I throw off the blankets and stand up to leave the room. At the door I turn back to see if she will give an answer. She is kneeling to pray with the pastel colors of the discarded blankets on one side. She is praying with her clasped hands resting on her lap, "thy kingdom come" she whispers, but I leave her there.

The next day they discover I can write as well as talk. Diotima comes up to my room and finds written all over my window in orange crayon, I HATE YOU MOMMY I HATE YOU MOMMY I HATE YOU MOMMY.

# Somniac

AND I am painting yellow streaks of watercolor on a white board and after each streak I rinse and rinse the color with clear water I rinse until the yellow is invisible and then I paint yellow streaks on the white board again. Diotima is not here with my mother and me today, she has gone to the sea.

...spray separates from the wave—at its tip twists off, spins distorted globes altering, by the wind's push met and kneaded, blown into shatters—spills silver on the rock...

...pieces of water fly landward in shuddering arcs splatter against the rock propelled unwillingly, elongating from the driving front, bulging away from the winding head to form before wasting, double-knobbed rods, splitting and falling on the rock, the water slashes against the rock and rises, whipped, slammed upward, smacked to suffocation, floundering, gripping air unsustained, froth at the windworn edges, bubbling coldseething flood, drips drops Diotima stands on the Atlantic on the beach in the March cold thinking. A day to be old in. Where is the other ocean, my ocean, an ocean without all these African skulls? Where is the Pacific? Where is Puerto Escondido? Where is my home? When shall I see the other ocean splash upon the stone caverns of Cinquetera, my home?

When the spray falls, it slaps the rock and then melts down the side returning; when the spray falls and leaves wet marks on the rock the sound is lonely. It is cold. Sometimes looking at the spray I am terrified.

The sea begins at the dark tips of her boots, the splotched leather napped and shrunk by water and rock, the sea begins at the sand that skirts the rock, sand woven in the calms a soft bend of earth, one sloping, it begins at hints of watery coming, the suck that drinks sea bottom into brine, the wave advancing, the slanted column of water racing toward the rock, it begins at the drop that drips, tumbles clumsy, the spray that lands on the rock.

There are pools of seawater, there are scoops that pocket ocean in sand, there are lashes that furrow, cilia that rage from the drowned sea heart to lick stings into the shore sieve earth, poisoned cups, and there is a driver of this drive. There are pools of seawater that even under clouds are white hard by day, silver by night, and they wait for the spray of the sea.

She turns from me, she turns. In the middle of my kiss she forgets. She smiles and turns her head softly to the window. Cuddling to me she smiles and speaks of the honey light in the window, how gentle and sweet. She asks for tea. She asks if I will sit in the light folding her in the comforter, softly. She plays with the golden fringe of her blouse. She leaves me.

And far and out, spluttering dim white, she whose toe is the black rock, whose chin is the rim of the horizon, she outspreads the water, her sunken head, her hair they are all the drowned sea heart, on her back she stretches southward toward another world. Her hips white watered, the bend of her knee kicks the spray.

And the cold comes through to my feet, it soaks through the soles of my boots, perhaps I stand on blocks of ice, perhaps my feet are naked against the ice. Cold, I have been standing in the cold a long time—long enough to have gone home by now. Long enough to have frozen to death here at the rock. I cannot see anything in this dark light, it splashes misty, I stand in an ice storm. I will return to Puerto Escondido. I will return to my father. There is nothing left for me here.

She turns from me. She turns.

And I could understand being alone now, I could understand never seeing her again. There is no glistening in the sand when the clouds are so thick and the sea puddling in the caved-in spots at the ends of waves—I am ashamed of my life, I am sad. There are no strange beasts in the puddles. The sea and I are empty. It drains quietly into the sand. I would not mind passion again. I never wanted to be this old, I never wanted my body to sag and sag—there is no passion left.

The sea goes far and sky and water are dim white, the horizon is a dim white thread.

There have been hot nights when I could not be satisfied. When I burned through the evenings...the spray awakes me from a fevered time, it tosses itself against me, I am old.

I think of the ecstatic time—remembering what? The gentleness of her face when she first showed up at the community center. The quiet beauty of her, a vacancy and shyness in her face, smooth cream beige marble, round face and fluffy hair. She was pregnant then with Johnnie, and running from her father...it took years for her to tell me that her father is Johnnie's father...years in which I, thinking I was her friend, companion, partner, became her servant, ordering the groceries, explaining to social workers at the front door that Johnnie need not be sent to school, lying beside her, Patricia, my Patricia, no not mine, never my lover, laying my hungry body beside her body those nights. She made love to me at the beginning, passion built up quietly in her until it reached some point...it had to overcome something in her, an aversion or abhorrence, passion would fall on her violently as if to blot out her abhorrence of human contact. Kisses to her are spit. Sexual moistness is slime and mucous until those moments when passion falls on her suddenly, dazzling her for a moment so that she forgets the vulgarity of the body's liquids...she thinks my body's liquids are vulgar. But how lovely she is when her face is flushed and she rocks her hips toward me and I feel her fingers on my breasts and between my legs. Patricia beloved. You have woven your spell over me carelessly. I must return to my community of mestizos in Puerto Escondido. I thought I could endure you, this country, the USAmericans, Patricia, Patricia is too much for me, the loveliest magnet. Sometimes I made her laugh, the picnic, we first made love at a picnic after Johnnie was born. In springtime, why not? Why shouldn't there be springtime sometime? her head thrown back in laughter. Her body weaving and fluttering over the grass—a butterfly? I have been aroused, I have given myself away, I have left everything for her, and now this splattering of cold drops and the sun no focus only a canopy of clouds, miserable, thick and thicker, an alien sky—I ache in my separate room now, and sometimes she gives me her blank unconscious kisses or leans on my shoulder—a beautiful dreamer. I sag. I am unfit.

I would not mind all day and all night to desire some special lips on my body, to desire, if it could be, someone I could have. Someone I choose and will not let go. Someone for me. I never won my lover. She never came to me though I rock and rocked her. I do not know anything except that I am old. It would be wonderful if even once now she came to me truly, if even once my desire caressing her body could call her to love and to a submersion in passion that comes gently, not violently, to imagine her giggling and hurrying to take off her clothes for me, to have her look at me when she feels sexual for me, to have her with me and not escaping me when I place my head between her legs. She is always so shocked when she looks up after orgasm, to discover that I am there, that someone is really there.

And look how the sides of the rocks are polished, preserved in ice. If the ice were a door I would walk through it and rest in the heart of it. I could be a statue waiting to be carved and there the spray would not torture me. I would stand in the rock undiscovered, I would flake away. How cold it is here.

I should have gone somewhere else. I should have gone home to my fogless beach. Puerto Escondido. Oaxaca. México. Another place. Another land. Where

101

this place would become that place. But I did not even think of it, it never even occurred to me, not after going to live with her. I must have been asleep. I'm going back home. I'm going back to México. This country can't have me anymore. Back home I'm going to tell them about these people. These people don't flow. Each one is a separate drop of water falling into a still pool, each drop waiting for stillness before it falls. And tomorrow is her father's birthday...their father's birthday. And I suppose she will celebrate it again.

Johnnie is seventeen now. Patricia and I were going to be lovers and parents. Johnnie is no child for me, no child with those white eyes, glittering white eyes in her black body and the insane dreamer, her mother. The insane dreamer her mother. Insane. Diotima stoops frightened, pierced pain in her chest. On the half frozen ground she lays her hand—all these years—her hand brushes against the dirty crystals, dirty crystals of frost still resting on the mud, cold, too much, too much cold. Johnnie. What an awful day it was when we found out that Johnnie could speak and read and write. Patricia screaming up in Johnnie's room, Johnnie sitting in a corner looking at her calmly, and across the picture window that looks down on the garden and the Potomac River Johnnie had written with an orange crayon, I HATE YOU MOMMY. Fourteen years old, and we just discovering that she understood everything. My little Johnnie. If only Johnnie were here. I wish I could take her to México.

Patricia never wanted me, she does not want me now. These years have been filled with her turnings away from me with a rustle of the sheets a sigh, her fingers forgotten—lingering on my body, she turns from me.

Landscape, melted ice and mudscape, and the wild brush wild and wrong. The winds drop down. There is nothing left to my spirit.

The sand changes color as each wave retreats from it. The water and foam move out and behind them a line ripples seaward from the sand, the line of saturation moves into the water, the drying line. It is so cold that some of the inward rocks are covered in ice. I should not stand here in the cold. The waters come between the rocks almost to my feet—I must leave to go back. I am cold. All these years. The sky has become more desolate than at first.

She gathers herself up, the toes of her boots wet with ice and cold, with seawater, gathers, picks herself up, tendon and bone, flesh, blood, Diotima gets up and comes back one more time. Fog, thick enveloping, a dirty white womb about her. "I love you. I love you. I love you!" Fog. Snow. Mud. She tries to look through the clouds. Where is the sun? I cannot find it. Everything is one deep cloud. At midafternoon I cannot tell where the sun has come from or where, what way it is going.

Something is dying.

Something is dying, Diotima. What are you going to do when you are alone? I think something is dying each time she turns from me, each time I think about death and I don't know what she is thinking. She does not listen, she goes away. She turns from me, she turns.

"Where's Diotima?"

gone out driving in the cold

Johnnie, slender and her dark fingers paint yellow streaks of watercolor on a white board then rinse out the watercolor to white, cross-legged on the floor, and whimpering at the window, March, the wind emptied itself, exhausted, tripping against itself, dipping into the hollows of the frantic Potomac, creeping lonely along the ground, fallen against the door.

"Where's Diotima?"

gone out somewhere in the car

"Johnnie, do you know where Diotima is?"

Johnnie said nothing. Johnnie who burnt the sun, burned black as martyrs, burned the sun, the ash, the coal in her flesh, and her eyes diamonds. Johnnie.

"Johnnie?"

Johnnie's face was empty. Johnnie's eyes were empty. Black. White. My thick nappy hair in knots and tangles, my eyes focused blankly on my mother. She gently pulls my hair back, looking into my light gray empty eyes, my harsh white eyes in my black face. "Johnnie, Johnnie." Nothing there, no answer, not the flicker of a sign, awaiting. "Johnnie, tell me what you're thinking."

I'm thinking about white painted boards.

# Afternoon

YELLOW watercolor on white boards. The three of them met again for the last time at the Potomac River on a March afternoon when the last of winter's snow and ice was breaking up in a fog.

I was painting yellow watercolor on white boards and repeating sad phrases to myself beginning with when. *When* and *if.*

When we get to heaven. If you get to heaven before I do. When shall we three meet again? If the chariot swings low. When you awaken. If you fall out of nightmare into rest. When the edge of the sea plushes the black rocks of the Allegheny Mountains in foam. If I just had two wings I would fly away to the kingdom.

On the afternoon my mother left me she wore a long silk lavender dress, with lavender skirts under it, and the bodice was embroidered in yellow and gold and golden orange, and the bands around her sleeves were embroidered also in bright gold. I was in my bedroom painting, thinning out a yellow color on a white board when she came to my door. She seemed about to leave, her fingers on the door anticipating, her eyes clear and intelligent and the dazed look was gone, all her movements were free. She came quickly into the room and kneeled beside me chattering and smiling, as if we were old friends, as if we had ever talked before. And I talked to her then—about my paintings, my rocks, my readings, my music. We were two conspirators planning an escape. We were two elegantly rich ladies scheduling tours and trinket tossing the places of the world. "And are you better then?" I asked her, "is the sorrow gone?" And she answered, "It's the beginning of something, Johnnie, a good thing is happening to me, it's time for us to leave this place, we've been brooding here too long. We're going to move. There's just too much in the world for us to be miserable here forever."

I laughed and laughed with my mother on the afternoon she left me as we played with journeys to far places. We talked about her sister Eva who lived across the bridge downtown in Washington, and we were going to go there and we talked about her other sister, Cynthia Jane, who was a nun in Villa Alva a Carmelite convent in Turkey Thicket by Catholic University and we were going to go there too we were going to go everywhere and there wasn't a shadow in her anywhere. "Let's have a picnic today Johnnie, let's celebrate, let's think of something to do—what does Diotima have? I'd like some peanut butter like when I was a kid do you eat peanut butter? Let's sit in the back garden for a while Johnnie and maybe later on we can walk over to the water I'd like to go for a walk." And jumping up from the floor she waltzed and fluttered over to the spattered window, lifted her hand happily and brushed her fingers against my mobile chimes, bent over my writing pad and played with an ink bottle, scraped her fingernail on my carved blue enamel box—all while I watched her from the floor. Her movements became quicker and more erratic, her fingers roved up and down among my things, not seeking but only touching, flicking, flickering, free and staccato, a lovely motion although strange, not circling but almost gyring around the room until she came to the mobile that hangs over the foot of my bed.

"Why do you have these bones here?" she asked softly. "They aren't bones, they are pieces of rock that were washed down the Potomac and I strung them together." "They're bones just the same." She was motionless, gently looking up at it. "All we have are bones left over from dead things." Her voice became hollow as she looked up and lifted her hand to the strung black pebbles.

"Do you think that it will snow again, Johnnie?" She turned again to me. "It snowed on the day I dropped out of school at Howard." She kneeled as a goddess with her skirts billowing around her and then settling, folding down in a soft woven pastel circle, facing my window, rain splatting against it, mist rising from the river, up the hill, to the roof. "I was at Howard University in Newman Hall, I was lingering after class and I saw the snow as it began.

"How can I explain it to you, Johnnie, you've never seen it and it was one of those moments, they happen sometimes in large buildings that so many people have been in and you know that because so many people have been there that somebody at some time must have been happy in there—it must have been so, there were so many people, but you are so unhappy as you stand there, and the building is empty yet the walls seem to echo because the air is cool and you know if you put your hand against the tile of the corridors it would be cold, standing there by the window, the thought that someone could have been happy there is a great mystery and the heat rising from the vent and the cool air from the window mixing together right there on my arm. And the Howard nursery school was just under the window and children were playing in the yard. And the way they were playing with the early snow and the gray air, I thought they were the first human beings on earth, Johnnie, they were so strange to me, and they were fighting a great battle just then, at the turn of winter. And the snow drifting in so slowly. They were digging in the sandbox to find something and laughing and dancing around it.

"That's when I knew I had to leave Howard. I was very lonely, Johnnie, I stood there fidgeting with the window, thinking of the long bus ride home and daydreaming of a flood—you see the clouds were so clear and thick they were outlined somehow like miles of foam on top of a wall of seawater that was going to fall down on Washington. And that's what the children were dancing about—except with the snow—perhaps the flood was already frozen. Before it even got to us.

"O Johnnie, forgive me, I had wanted a place where the light was bright and the thickness of the air dispersed. I had wanted to see clearly."

And then more softly, my mother, the beautiful one said, "I am tired of wandering among these shadows."

"What is it, Mother?"

"But now I'm going to be happy. I'm going to walk down to the river. Today's my Daddy's birthday and I want to think about him and everybody how we were back at home, today I want to remember everything, I'll be back before nightfall, it's about two o'clock now, and perhaps I'll only stay by the water an hour or so just tell Diotima that I'm feeling pretty good today and I'll be home before nightfall, my Johnnie...

...and my mother Patricia walked through the cold rain down to the Potomac danced to the Potomac through the late misty ice storm bounced down toward the slick icy Potomac to look out over the March water half-water half-ice melting under rain the March waters cold luminous gray misty complaining swollen from the mountains clogged trees boxes cans a drowned dog loosening and descending cold waters tearing away the heart from around Three Sisters Island through the city churning and breaking the ice in streaks of wet dark light the Potomac knobby with plant stuff muddy thick and I, Johnnie, secretly sadly came following after...

...and my mother Patricia turned her back to the Potomac and raised her arms toward Washington City she raised her arms in the cold the icy falling water caressed her so beautiful she was happy when she began to raise her arms she raised them because she was happy as she lifted them above her hips, her waist, she was happy her stomach her breasts happy or something else happy or maybe not happy maybe something kin to it but greater wider lovelier sweeter above her neck something beyond everything else something called other names something wider deeper...

...and my mother Patricia raised her arms toward her sisters and her sisters came to her from out of the City of Washington, from Rock Creek and Anacostia they came to Patricia upon the Potomac, Cynthia Jane and Eva, and those three met again above Three Sisters Island above the Potomac with my mother who raised her arms above her face her hair her embrace held the city her invocation of Washington in her happiness it was freedom there was nothing else only the moment of happiness it flushed her cold body threw back her head loved her in the sparkling rain she tried to think of a name she wanted a name for it prayed for a name she would stand there until she found a name and that name was joy yellow whip sting singed desolate laugh forsaken, it was her name, her heartbeat, patPat patPat prettyPat patPat and after she spoke that name she turned back to the Potomac still raging around the island tearing away the city screeching sucking itself from between clumps of ice flinging itself raging down again toward the Tidal Basin, the Chesapeake Bay toward the sea breaking and the three sisters moved in a circle singing...

...and my mother Patricia forgot the city of Washington forgot Georgetown and Sixteenth Street and Rock Creek Park and Eastland Gardens and Anacostia, forgot Mayfair Mansions and Kenilworth and Deanwood and Parkside and Capitol Heights, forgot River Terrace and Langston and Benning Heights and Turkey Thicket, forgot F Street and the Carnegie Library, forgot her home forgot everything she was there with the river, and the Potomac deep in eye and lung was eye and lung breather and breath were the Potomac her flesh rushed through her pores eastward and the splotchy patch that remained hovering point at the water surface, unraveled into the horizon dispersed utterly...

...and stretching her right hand first toward her sisters and then to heaven, she dissolved above the churning Potomac River...

...and seeing her, Diotima rushed from the path beside the Whitehurst Freeway and over the muddy slush to the rough waters, battled the waters, dashed and beaten toward the ice she reached toward the death hole there leaning she grabbed my mother's clothes and for an instant my mother's crushed face exposed skull in flash of water light dashed toward her before the great pull took over and the water carried my mother away dragging her toward the Atlantic...

please mommy no, no no, I wept toward heaven, mommy take me don't leave me o no, ono don't leave me mommy, I want to go with you,
don't leave me
but she left me
don't don't don't leave me mommy
she was gone
don't don't don't leave me mommy mommy mommy
but she had struck her skull, she had caved in her face on stone she dropped like the click of a clock, that tap of a cat on a wooden floor, she walked down the tall steps of Georgetown and stepped out above the Potomac River...

...and Diotima heard my cries and feared she would lose us both in the same day preserve, preserve the child Diotima scraped and abraded in the airless place she worked her way back let me get to the child in time unfleshed and kneaded gasping along the base of the rock she whimpered and grabbed herself along

...and my moaning was louder than the river exhausted at the shore Diotima heard my disconsolate moaning grief agony mourning losing my lost mother

# D'n'C

MOMMY! Mommy! Mommy! Up the stairs. Mommy! Mommy! Mommy! Mommy! Mommy! Run up the stairs run. Raining. Hurry. Run, Johnnie, run quick. To Eva. Run to your Aunt Eva. You remember how I told you if anything happens and you don't know what to do. You know how I told you. I showed you the street. Remember Johnnie. Go and find P Street where I pointed it out to you and keep on walking on P Street until you get to Logan Circle. Please Johnnie before the police get here try to remember how I told you. There will be two circles. They're like streets that go in a circle. The first one is called Dupont Circle. Go on around Dupont Circle until you get to P Street again. There's another P Street that leaves from the other side. And keep on walking until you get to another circle. That's called Logan Circle. Go to the big white house on Logan Circle and tell Eva what happened. It's the biggest white house on the circle sitting all by itself with streets on both sides of it and ask for Eva. It's your Aunt Eva, Johnnie. That's where she lives. Don't be afraid, Johnnie. You'll have to walk on the cement sidewalk. If you get there Eva will take care of you. Run Johnnie. Run fast.

Mommy! Mommy! Mommy! Mommy! Mommy! Police. Mommy! Run. Run. Up the stairs. Remember. Up. Home down there. No. Not home. M Street. The other way. M Street. Thirty-fifth Street. N Street. Cross Thirty-fourth Street. Thirty-third Street. Cross O Street. Run. Keep running. Don't get tired. Can't get tired. Tired of running. Mommy! Alone. Alone on the street. Raining. Raining on

109

me. First time alone on the street. Run. P Street. I made it to P Street. This is P Street. I can read it, P Street. I found it. I found it. Wisconsin Avenue. P Street. Neams Market. Chocolate Shoppe. This is the way Diotima showed me. This is the way Diotima pointed me. This way is Washington City. This is the way Diotima walked me to show me. Washington. Presbyterian Congregational Church. Down here. Run. I can't run any longer. Keep running. Run quick. Thirty-first Street. Drip. A tree. Dripping on me. Mommy! Mommy! Raining on me. Blowing on me cold. Mommy! Mommy! Mommy! Mommy! Mommy! Mommy! Mommy! Willow tree. Diotima told me. Willow tree. Run. Cross Dumbarton Rock Court West Lane Keys Thirtieth Street the antique shop. The antique shop where Diotima brought me. Remember. I remember. It was here. Brown wood furniture shiny. Stuff brown full crowded pretty. In there. China. Bronze. Made of bronze sign hanging awning green awning nice. There. Remember. Remember run. Run quick Johnnie, run quick. Run. Cross Twenty-ninth Street run the Old House the old Christmas wreaths around the round hole of the old garden entrance of the Old House 1863 run the Griffin Market there. There. There. There they are. Those strange buildings. Over there is Washington. That's where it is. Over there. Over there where they don't have brick sidewalks Twenty-seventh Street. Curving like water. Georgetown Liquor Store. Georgetown Thrift Shop. Georgetown rain Twenty-sixth Street. Mannequins. Diotima told me. Those aren't alive. Across run across here's the playground. Wet. Rock Creek and Potomac Parkway. Strange buildings. Diotima brought me here. She brought me this far. Right here. Here. Where the brick sidewalk stops. Step over. I can't. I don't know how. Step over. I never stepped over before. Mommy and Diotima told me, Johnnie, don't ever step over. Don't step off the brick sidewalk. Run down P Street. I can't. The sidewalk changes. Step.

Cement. Stop running. Walk. Walk down P Street. Here's P Street Bridge. And Rock Creek flowing under it and curving down toward the Potomac. The mist rises from it so softly, blue and soft, and where's my mother?

How many times have I stood back there and looked at that white church? And the statue of the soldier on the horse. I could barely see it. And now it's right over there. And those strange buildings are right in front of me, right beside me, because now I'm in Washington City. This is it. This is the place. This is that place. Twenty-third Street. Different apartments. Different stores. Different hotels. Cement sidewalks. Performing Arts Store. Twenty-first Street. Health Club. Twentieth Street. A black face screaming to himself as he walks down the street. Power to the people. Power to the people. Gotta git power goddammit to hell we need power Second Story Books, Dupont Circle. People and people and people.

A burned black and white face. I walk around until I find the other P Street. Here it is. Buildings are different over here but I don't know how exactly. Are they bigger? No! We have big houses in Georgetown. But not big like this. This is different. American Trucking Association. Sixteenth Street. Foundry Methodist. Carnegie Institute. I have to keep walking until I come to another circle. I'm tired. My legs are tired and I'm all by myself. I wonder why Diotima sent me here. I wonder why she told me to walk over here. I'm very cold and wet and tired. And I don't know where I'm going. I have to keep going. This is a long way. Fifteenth Street. Look. Look down there. It's the Washington Monument way down there. Look at it. A smooth white column with a point on top.

"Hey sugaaaah!"

The Washington Monument.

"Hey sugaaaah baby doll sweetheart dahlin'—I like yo' style but yuh gots tuh git outa thuh street honey chile."

Right down there. But I have to keep walking down P Street until I come to another street that goes in a circle. Car Wash. Brake Service. Columbia Lighthouse for the Blind. Kill White Parasites. Support Your Community Theater Company. Die Nigger. Fuck the State. Black People Unite. Your Slop Shop. Play Hard Die Young. Do it. Video Games. The American Dream Is The World's Nightmare. Pawnbroker. Fourteenth Street.

"C'mon, wouldja git out muh way, can'tja see I'm tryinuh git my...doan push on thuh...where's my...didja see muh...what thuh fuck...hey, fool, you got sum...damn it, sucker, git off my heels, Jeezuss...you know I don't hang wit' no shit like that...great god in Zion whut have we here...hey, babeee! You new on thuh street? Hey, now, it's gonna bee awright! Where'd jooo cum from baby, you need a lover? Sweet thang!...you talk about a black stack...you somethin' else honey chile...when thuh berry's that black an' round you know the juice be done gots tuh be sweeeeet...where in thuh world did joo cum frum...you got sum funky eyes, didja see them eyes...I'm seein' as much as I kin an' would by the grace of almighty god that I might pinch a piece of that precious puss...c'mon fool, layoff, cantja see she ain't no D.C. nigger? She don't know what thuh hell you talkin' bout...where do you cum from? she's a brick house, o lord ain't she...she's mighty mighty...lawd, that I wuz a young fool one more time...yeah she's a brick house, she's mighty mighty an' she's lettin' it all hang out...Where do you come from?"

Georgetown.

"Whut? Georgetown? Ya'll hear that? Chile say she cum frum Georgetown. Well sweeteebaby ya'll sho' look like Georgia an' Alabama to me! will ya'll shut the fuck up while I talk to thuh child?! Ain't no nigger that black cum from Georgetown...whut thuh hell are you talkin' 'bout fool, shit! they got niggers in Georgetown. The hell they do. Them ain't real niggers. They's Africans. But I'm talkin' 'bout black niggers. An' anyhow, Africans ain't no kinda niggers at all. Aw shut up fool you don't know shit! But them eyes, somethin' dun snuck through there, them sure ain't no African eyes nor no black eyes neither."

"I apologize for my brothers here, they don't mean any harm."

What are they saying?

"They're saying that you are very beautiful."

Would you thank them for me?

"Certainly."

But don't they speak English? Doesn't everyone here speak English?

"No."

Do you know how far Logan Circle is?

"It's right down here, just two blocks. You can see it."

I have to go to my Aunt Eva's house.

"Eva? Do you mean Eva Snowdon?"

Yes, my Aunt Eva, Snowdon is her last name.

"Really? I know her. She's one of our patrons up here at the theater where I work, Source Theater. I've been to her house lots of times—she gives a lot of parties for theater people. I can show you where it is. You've never been there? Can I walk you over there?"

Kingman Place. A short street on one side. And there's the street in a circle. Logan Circle. How misty and rainy it is. So dark and blue. I've walked all the way here. My mother's way back there carried away by the Potomac River. My mother left me. A statue. Logan. Logan. And there's that tower way up there. Way up there. I bet it's that same tower. Is that the same tower? The tower on my calendar at home. I wonder. Founder's Library of Howard University. Yes, that's Howard University. My grandfather was up there. I wonder. So rainy. This is my aunt's house. The big one here. Right across from the smaller one that says Tourist Home. My aunt's house. I'm going in.

# Chiaroscuro

SHE is a virgin. She rubs her eye and notices the chill in the room. The room is a small dark box hanging around her. Her left hand is resting on her left leg near the knee, looking for warmth. She remembers to relax her face. She smells the mild stink of her body rising from her feet and from between her legs. She has been too lethargic to bathe herself. She does not want to think about her mother anymore. She wants to rest, to sleep. The walls of the room creak as the pipes fill with steam heat. She sits brooding as once her mother sat brooding. Now she wants to lie down in a bed and sleep. If only she could sleep. She wonders what it would be like. Once upon a time she saw her grandfatherfather make love to her mother with his hand. She moves her hand.

An airplane flies above the house. There is a war coming or already come. She smells the cold tea from the cup and winces against the cold taste of it in her mouth. Her tongue touches her teeth. Dirty. There is a pause of nothing in her mind.

A car passes. She looks out of the window. She scratches her head and sighs. Her mind becomes even more quiet. Mute. Forsaken. The Story of the Stone. Daddy. The King of Hearts.

There is slush in the streets and a white bird curves over the Potomac River. Then there are several birds. She is filled with silence and chill. The flock of white birds turns and reels over the Potomac River. She does not see them. Her body is touched with weariness that cannot rest, no place of peace.

She looks out of the other window where the snow rims the dark edges of the heavy, moving branches. "Should I go out walking?" but her shoulders slump as she bends toward the window. Someone is crossing the street from snow to snow in the street slush. A person or a dog blotted out by the branches of the trees. Someone who has not yet left for the mountains. "Mommy." She cries out. She wants to forget her mother. Chalice. Afternoon.

Someone on a bicycle passes going the other way. "Before I had my eyes put out I liked as well to see..." But her eyes have not been put out. She has no choice but to see. It was a dog who had crossed the street, dark against the snow and running. She cannot stop thinking of her mother. The First Time.

The curve of the bridge that crosses the Potomac between Rosslyn and Georgetown frames nothing. The sky that left the snow is clearing into blue and white. She glances at her mat and blanket and pillow on the floor. A place upon which to lie awake forever. The heater is not on.

She stands to turn on the heater and passes herself in the mirror. Stretches with her arms up, and again smells her body. Sits. Stretches again and shudders. Nothing. No one. No rest. No mother. Just a small dark box in an empty city to live in forever.

At the table she rests her head in her hands. "Why have I remained here?" A room alone in the city. The river flows southward between the icy shores. She is cold.

She sips the cold tea and frowns. Then she stands up to put water on to boil. She washes a large cup and a silver spoon. What would it be like to rest? To lie down in a bed and sleep? To die before I wake. I want to sleep and die before I wake.

She pours the powder of instant soup into the cup and throws the paper into the trash bag.

She sits and puts on her white sweater, closes her eyes...rubs her right eye again, blinking, closes her eyes and feels nauseated from so much cold tea.

She looks through the other window and debates whether to go out. The water begins to hiss on the stove behind her. "How am I to choose?" Faerie Tale. Another Faerie Tale. A snow-plow passes by in the street.

It snowed so long and is melting so quickly. And the birds are slivers of blue ice over the icy river. It has been over ten years since her mother stepped into the Potomac. She does not want to think about it anymore. She thinks about it. D'n'C. Dilatation and Curettage. DC. Washington.

The sun works its way through the clouds slowly, she feels a warm current of air against her leg and cheek. So many birds. The teakettle whistles. Never to have fallen asleep. Never to escape, to rest. "Mommy." Always to be god's holy black virgin. Mommy's bundle. To be condemned to consciousness, knowledge, vision. To be condemned to immortality. Never to be permitted to die. To forget never. To live forever. Somniac.

114

She stands and turns and walks to the stove, turns off the heat, and pours the boiling water over the powdered soup in the cup. She stirs the cup with her silver spoon. She returns to the table with the cup of soup in one hand and the hot teakettle in the other. She pours the remaining hot water into the standing teapot with its cold tea and then returns the kettle to the stove.

At the table, sitting in her chair, she sips the lukewarm tea. She looks at the cup of soup. She stands and walks back to the kitchenette, lifts her left hand and opens the white cabinet. With her right hand she takes out a small plate to place under the hot cup of soup on the small wooden table. The Last Time.

The smell of hot instant chicken noodle soup rises over her face. The cup is hot in her hands. The silver spoon is too hot to touch.

As she begins to eat the soup the chill of rising body heat passes through her. Her insides shudder and tremble, her shoulders, the muscles at the base of her neck relax. Even more. No thought or comfort to warm her body.

She is hunched over the cup. "Should I read something?" She is remembering the long walks she took when she first learned Washington, after that March afternoon when she ran from Georgetown to Logan Circle. "I stayed with my Aunt Eva until May that year. Now the years are gone. It is another late winter. Almost all the black folk have accepted the compromise and gone to the mountains. Their lives are safe there, THEY have agreed not to bomb out THEIR fellow third-world people if they go to the enclaves. But I cannot leave. There were always towers and steeples at first. And the Sestren at the convent. And my grandmother's tale of her Pianoforte. And the walk to My Grandparents' Door. And my grandmother's Love for me.

"My Aunt Eva. It was too much. And later that year my Aunt Sister Cynthia Jane whose skin is black as my skin is black. I think I don't want to think." She bends over the soup and eats. "And my grandfatherfather. And my grandmother." She fills the teacup again with lukewarm tea. "I saw them all then." She raises her face to the window where the sky is becoming brighter. So quiet the city, as if it has fallen asleep after a long nightmare. She drinks the tea from her Italian teacup—antique white with red-pink flowers and green leaves and gold, gold that reminds her of her Aunt Eva.

The house where I arrived was large and beautiful after the run from Georgetown in the rain. But after all, nowhere to get to. Nowhere to run. And the house in Georgetown, nowhere to run from. "But this room. Now." In the back corner her pile of clothes awaits sorting. Dirty.

This is a room to think in. It has no river, it is away from the Potomac River and it is away from space. It has no extra space. It is small and crowded. The Potomac River is in her mind only. She cannot see it. She is in a narrow dark apartment at Seventh and K. Imagining her Georgetown room above the river. She is confined in the room, blocked in. "Mommy! Where is my..." She eats the soup. She chews a reconstituted chunk of dried chicken. She drinks tea. She gulps the soup from the spoon quickly. "Where is my mother?

"My neck hurts." She gulps more soup. She pours more tea. The bridge that spans the Potomac River between Rosslyn and Georgetown reflects the sunlight.

She drinks the tea. "I have a lot of clothes to wash. And dishes. I feel so warm inside, and lethargic—so happy in my quiet room."

Her room is at the top of a narrow house. She has a moment of perfect quiet. Sometimes she speaks aloud. "I am subject to dreams and fantastic visions. I have seen Enoch striding upon the stars." She came to the Washington Hilton from Benning Heights. She scratches her scalp, then places her hand again on the warm cup. Her hair is dirty. She drinks the soup.

The sun breaks through absolutely. She drinks the soup. The sunlight accents the trees, the buildings, chimneys. Soup. And touches the decorative cement ball standing above the wall next to the wrought-iron gate. Sunlight.

How she desires to sleep as she looks out at the snow. A runner jogs by under the window. "Mommy, Mommy, Mommy." She calls out. She finishes the soup.

She places the plate with the soup up on the table. "She hugged me sometimes in the beginning. I wonder what it would have been like to have slept by now. My mother loved my grandfatherfather. I grew up in Georgetown.

"I wish I could pull down the shades and fall asleep on the couch. Or on my mat on the floor. To sleep in the snow. The couch is small and cramped. For daytime. The mat is for night. I have all those clothes piled in the corner.

"I need a bath. I need to wash myself. Oh, Mommy! I've had enough. How can I sit here any longer?" Silence. Spring Mourning.

Blood drains down from her head through her body, her complacent body. No confrontation, it is enough. The bitter dry taste of instant chicken noodle soup adds to the other old tastes in her mouth. She should wash her teeth. She should move. She should do something.

She descends into hell. She looks out of the other window. The lamp has become irrelevant in the sunlight.

There is a candle scent in the room left over from last night. Bayberry. "Let me sleep. They're fussing again. Who's fussing? Who? Mommy and Daddy? Who? Who? Mommy and Diotima. But I don't *have* anything to say. But I *really* don't have anything to say. I always hear voices interrupting everything I think.

"I can't remember. I wasn't there. Or I was too young, or something. Who put the light in the library? Why don't you let me sleep?" Now you are a light. Johnnie. A clear light in an empty skull.

You are a light remembering, imagining between a night and a morning, a winter's day. Journal. Three Witches. Monopoly. Atlantis. Someone moves across the lawn on the other side of the street wearing cross-country skis. "Where am I? Who's calling me? Who's calling me?" Chiaroscuro.

*Light*—the marble, the ice, the fields, the rooftops. *Dark*—the sidewalks, the streets, the trees, the water. "And the towers. The towers of St. Matthew's Cathedral and the towers of the Smithsonian Castle, the towers of the Throne of the Third Heaven, the tower of the Old Post Office Pavilion, the tower of the Shrine of the Immaculate Conception, the towers of the National Cathedral—all light, and the tower obelisk of George Washington. What happened? It was slavery. And white and black are so close. And dark and light are so close. And someone's white grandfather buried someone's black grandfather after those slaves sang that song and died. Truth. Freedom. They wouldn't go back, no, not back to the South. It was slavery that happened and I read the story in a book.

"Who buried whom? Is the story over? Those two nations. Africa and Europe. The lord prepared an enemy, a great adversary, one for the other." She sneezes, the room is so cold. "There were two nations fighting in a single womb, each striving to kill the other, they came to America, and fell as one into sleep, dream, nightmare, upon the Potomac River. They shall awaken into death.

"David Bradley wrote the story. The people he wrote of were cooking in the mountains. Black folk. And everyone went to the mountains. That's where the black folk have gone, that's why the city is empty. And all the black children are gone from Clifton Terrace and Anacostia and everywhere. Don't you understand? THEY, that is, all the third-world nations, are in a war against US, the United States, and no person of color can fight for US. So in the compromise THEY agreed with US that if the black folks go to the mountains, the Alleghenies, THEY won't drop bombs on the Alleghenies. That's why I'm here alone and the city is empty. The war has come, and the white males have gone off to fight. But the black folk have all gone up to the mountains. The black folk go to the farther side of the mountain where the trees are so much thicker. Then everyone is there living together along the mountains, but clinging to those mountains, afraid, as if Dante's Satan had formed that mountain when he fell, the trees stiff hairs of his legs.

"The Alleghenies are all that's left of Satan's hair. And you must climb Satan's hairy legs to reach paradise. Only a remnant left of black folk. A scattered people hiding in the mountains. My body smells. I need hot water, I need to wash my body in hot water. History doesn't help. Slavery won't go away.

"And all the cards that make up history. Sibylline leaves, leaves of Vallombrosa, leaves of Dumbarton Oaks around the pond washing up by seawater receded where I walked with Diotima and my mother.

"I can't find my way out. It is too late to find my way out when they have gone. How could it possibly be done? What happened? Slavery happened. Africans came into bondage to Europeans in a new promised land. And males with light, bright, white skin slept with the black females who had nursed them, and slept with their sisters, and slept with their daughters and nieces and cousins and begot children—and thus began a great crime of these contending peoples of

117

one nation. The dark, black, brown skinned boys were killed or sold so as not to interrupt the white masters, and the girls were trained up into sexual slavery to the masters. Slavery happened. But why should they all leave the place where we should have been together? Why am I living here, so cramped? What do I want to figure out?

"The Throne of the Third Heaven is a room of tin foil and words that no one can read and I want to read them. I want to understand. Who is left alive? How much time has passed since I decided to come here and to lie on the sofa from time to time and wonder what it would be like to rest? And wonder what it would be like to sleep. The city, the city is around me.

"Diotima left me. After they found and cast my mother into the Atlantic Diotima went to México. I stayed with Aunt Eva for a while. After my mother left me I met everyone for the first time, Eva, Cynthia Jane, Camille, John Christopher. I never knew them before. They had to tell me everything. I don't know what they were like before my mother left me. They all talked to me except Diotima. Where is Diotima? Now I am alone in the city. Solitude. The sun has gone in again. They all left me. My mother left." She blows her nose on a scrap of toilet paper. She has no tissue.

And sits gazing out of the window with the dirty paper in her hand. Now she is a light. In the Children's Room. In the Young Adult Room. Now she is a light.

In the second-floor hallway, marble and wood and brass. Now she is a light in the Old Carnegie Public Library of Washington, D.C. At the window. She coughs. The stairway. She coughs again and turns her body on the cramped sofa. Come down, down to the first floor. This city is over, that was once full of people. This place. That place.

Straight ahead a large wooden doorway and a card catalog. To the left the room where they keep *Paradise Lost*. To the right the room where they keep maps of Washington, D.C. Turn and go down. Come down. Come down. Straight ahead the cabinet of pictures. This is where they all learned to read. This is where they understood what would happen, that they would become a wild people living in the mountains, uncouth fortune-tellers called on to prophesy in times of drought and famine. This is where they came on Saturday when my Grandmother Camille was working at Third Baptist Church. Now all of them are gone. Black folk. Gone.

To the left the Art Room and the Music Room. She walks along the side where the most recent records are stacked in open cabinets. Dark pictures, shadowy portraits, are on the wall. She sits in a booth. The city is empty. Flat top. Round top. Pointed top. Lincoln. Jefferson. Washington. Empty. She puts on earphones. This little light of mine.

The toilet paper drops from her hand. She leans forward and listens.

This little light of mine,
I'm gonna let it shine.
This little light of mine,
I'm gonna let it shine
Well now this little light of mine,
I'm gonna let it shine
Let it shine, let it shine, let it shine

Oh Freedom, Oh Freedom
Oh, Freedom over me my Lord
And before I'd be a slave
I'd be buried in my grave
And go home to my Lord
And be...

a light

# Love

10/2/99

DEAR Johnnie, I wish you would come up to the mountains. The truce may not last and you may not be safe there in Washington. Also I think it must be too sad for you there. Here we have decided to organize our community more thoroughly, assuming that we will never be able to move back to the city.

Should I send anything? Any food or supplies down to you? What do you need? I'm worried that you don't have the right things to eat. The supplies are solid here, not only because the truce lets the transports come in, but actually we've become better at taking care of ourselves. A lot of the thing I learned in order to teach science come in handy now. We've put everything we know together so we can grow decent vegetables and we know how to make clothes from animals and plants. It's not so bad, and we have one whole group interested in weaving, their work gets more and more refined.

Of course I still grieve over Patricia and I know you do too. Sometimes the thoughts of it all make me quite weak and sad, although I know I'm strong in spite of it. I know I can bear it. You mustn't think of me as being destroyed by all of this. I'm worried more about you, Johnnie, I don't know how to worry about myself anymore. If you can come through all of this, to be well in your mind and your body, then I'll be satisfied—I'll be victorious. I want you to do more than survive, I want you to triumph! I want you to triumph not only over the crimes our family committed against you and against one another, I want you to triumph

120

over the evil life you have to live in that evil city. I never thought I would be able to give up my family and my city so easily, all of my family except you. I send you my love again and again Johnnie, and hope you'll be able to escape Washington somehow, and all its harm. You should come here with us.

I keep feeling afraid that the truce may not hold long enough for the retreat. They could attack the cities. I don't think Washington is safe. Sometimes I wish we had all gone to México like Diotima. We've heard rumors that it's pretty safe on the Pacific from Puerto Escondido southward—it's only Acapulco and northward that have trouble.

We've heard about that case in Virginia by the way. What has the world come to if they can arrest a black couple just for trying to get married? As if it were our fault only white males fought the war. And now that most of them are dead we have to put up with this new law or come up here to the mountains. I'm told that they may try to enforce the law even up here, so that black couples won't be allowed to have children. What will become of us—we who are black and female—if parenthood is reserved for white mothers and black fathers? It's an evil law to keep this nation as white as possible, and as for black mothers, they think we might as well be eliminated.

You're my only grandchild. In spite of all our troubles I was glad when you finally came to visit us in Washington. And didn't you enjoy that trip you made with me and the school kids! Land and water forms of Washington, D.C. You hadn't really seen the whole city before then in spite of the time you spent with Eva and Janie. You came to me last of all but I can understand that. And then you spent so much time talking to John Christopher that it was a while before you and I could talk. How you laughed when I taught you how to recognize the monuments to the three presidents: Washington has a pointed top, Jefferson has a round top, Lincoln has a flat top. And that was all ten years ago.

We have all had to live such a sad life. I could never have imagined it considering how happy I was growing up in Kenilworth. It seems every day now I spend some time remembering how life was before I met John Christopher. My aunt and I lived at the end of a very long street, Douglass Street, and there was a District Grocery Store on the corner of Douglass Street and Kenilworth Avenue. I guess I walked up that street to that store every day of my life, sometimes with barely a nickel, just to be doing something. I had a dog named Prince who must have been the smartest dog in the world. Once Prince saved the life of the little boy across the street by smacking his hand every time the little boy tried to pick up a rattlesnake. Everybody praised Prince that day, especially the boy's father, who was ready to go after Prince with a stick until he saw the snake. I was really proud of Prince, so happy—but I have to admit that there are times now when I wonder what it was all for. I wanted such a happy life for all of my children.

I haven't gotten over anything, all the good things that were and how they changed. I still don't understand how Patricia became the way she was. I knew something was wrong when she was about two years old. There was a hurricane in Washington, Hurricane Carol, and it actually knocked the steeple off one of the churches downtown. In the middle of the storm I found her petrified and soaked at the window. A tree had fallen—you know Rock Creek Park was right across the street. She had been watching the storm blowing the treetops. Her right hand had frozen to the glass of the window that was raised up above her head. It was so strange—it seemed as if she had been struck by lightning just as she had reached up to pull down the window. She was catatonic. Perhaps the thunder had frightened her so. She was soaked through to the skin. I couldn't bend her arms and legs at all and when I picked her up she went into an X shape and wouldn't come out of it. I tried to soothe her—John Christopher told me she would be all right and I didn't have to take her to the hospital but I always blame myself for that. She was so different afterwards, after she woke up from that trance. I should have taken her to the hospital anyway. It was after that when she started to show those strange feelings for John Christopher. And yet how could a storm have done that? It's as if she had been raped by a hurricane.

So much has failed me and yet I feel such hope for our people here in the mountains and particularly for you, Johnnie. So much failed me—my love for John Christopher failed me. But at least love has happened once for me, Johnnie. I thought my love for John would die when I knew he and your mother were together. I lived in hell. It was an awful morning when Janie and I saw Eva in the hospital and we knew that John Christopher and Patricia were in San Juan together. What a morning that was. A terrible night and a morning worse than two yesterdays. Janie and I ate breakfast. Patricia in San Juan. And the phone call came about Eva. Life in hell. But love has happened once to me although I could not save them with it. But then no one gets to save anybody! I've learned that if nothing else. No one ever gets to save anybody! No one gets to keep anybody, no one gets to own anybody, no one gets to save anybody. You can help, encourage, sacrifice for, and love somebody. Yes, Johnnie, you can love somebody. But you cannot save anybody. No. I wanted so much to save my family.

The coldest day. I lost my mind for a while that day. On the way to the hospital with Janie driving, I went mad. What happens to love when there is so much evil? To love John Christopher while he was involved in such evil drove me to madness. I had always secretly agreed with Job's wife as to what to do in catastrophe, why not curse God and die? When your home and your life fall apart why not curse love and leave? But what could I say about the love that had been there before? Could I say it never existed? If it had never existed there was good cause for the evil that came afterwards. But there was no good cause for that evil. And love, yes, love had happened once for me, Johnnie, although its joy left me.

Love is independent. I keep an idea how John Christopher was when I first knew him, and I've imagined how we could have grown toward each other—the image is so beautiful and could have been true. The idea stays with me and makes the terrible things that happened even sadder. I imagine that even John kept an idea of how his original love for me and our children would grow, and that idea was good. A memory that would finally drive him mad. My idea of love gave me power to turn from him to my solitude. How I turned from him!

I helped Patricia to live in Georgetown, protected her by hiding from John Christopher where his money to support her was going. And I told him to leave Patricia alone when he wanted to give her an abortion. I ask myself now why I did not leave him altogether.

He raped her. I discovered he had raped her. That first time. He finally told me. They took a bath together. He hates baths because they leave a film on the skin. He put her to bed and showered off the film. When he came to bed she was asleep, sound asleep! He walked around and around that room for an hour, watching her sleep, making noises to wake her, she did not awaken. She had tried to seduce him and after all did not want him. Not even once. She fell asleep. He raped her. It was not coercion from Patricia but rape from her father. And it has been my fate to live long enough to know this and not die.

And I lived long enough for him to leave me. I wanted to recover something, restore, redeem something. I wanted to salvage something and bring just a little peace to our home. I have always thought that although no one can be purely good, if we could each try to pass on less evil than we received we would finally redeem the world. This is the idea that has kept me strong all these years. Pass on less evil than you receive. I had believed that before we parted John Christopher and I would be friends. But he left me. He did not want to salvage love with me and his guilt was too great to allow reconciliation. No one gets to save anybody. Yet the original idea of love still has not forsaken me. I am foolish. I don't know how to fall out of love. And they burned his body, as much as he feared burning they still cremated him.

And will you stay there and keep brooding over your mother and our family? Washington is no help anymore. "The strong give up and move on, the weak give up and stay"—it's from some song they've been singing here. Will you ever give up and move away? I wish I could know what it was exactly that made Patricia so unhappy. I've never been able to account for it although I think over and over the old things. Certainly that hurricane wasn't enough to explain it—that just lets me know that something was wrong as early as that, before she was six years old. It seems to me that something is hidden from me. Some people I've talked it over with talk about her being a genius, as if somehow a genius is supposed to be sick and strange. It's true that she was quite gifted—perhaps a genius—but I could never understand how genius would explain how miserable she would feel at times when she was growing up. She told me many, many times that she hated the earth, she hated life and wanted no part of it. She told me she wanted to die. It is an awful thing to hear words like that from my own child.

When I asked her why she felt that about life she would start talking about herself as if she were a myth, a myth of a falling city, or nation, or world, or god. She ran away from home once when she was in junior high school—the police found her curled up under a bush down on the Mall near where they built the East Building Annex of the National Art Gallery. When I went down to pick her up at the Children's Bureau she told me she had picked that spot because it represented the art of the falling city and nation—but I'm convinced she curled up just there because it was the closest spot to the police station. She wanted to be found as soon as possible—and the fact that she went down there and did that in the first place and then wanted to be found so quickly meant to me that she was trying to tell us something. The note she left for me before she went down there said she was going to "where pixies play and faeries dwell." I thought she meant she was going to the library and it took hours for me to realize that something was wrong. Something. And I guess that something stayed wrong because I was never able to figure out what she was trying to tell us. I took her to a psychologist recommended by the school counselor but then Patricia kept calling the psychologist stupid—and to tell the truth I thought she wasn't very helpful, just kept giving Patricia these psychological tests that didn't have any answers. John Christopher and I decided to put Patricia in another school and the problem seemed to go away for a while. It went away for a while but came back with a vengeance when she started trying to seduce John Christopher.

And Johnnie, are you reliving all these horrors? Washington is too painful for you, all the earthly griefs we suffer are larger there in the city, it's no wonder you hear voices. Love can calm those voices, Johnnie. And it's not possible that you've seen wolves crossing the Potomac. You have imagined it, it's not true. Wolves are wonderful beautiful animals and not devils. Many beautiful beings have been eliminated from the world, destroyed because someone decided that they are devils, don't believe that wolves are devils.

Don't brood about the Potomac. There is no bag lady living in the river. And from the way you describe the location of your room you can't see the river anyway. I'm glad that you haven't moved back to Georgetown. Your room sounds terribly small, I suppose it's one of those apartments over a store, there aren't really any houses on that part of Seventh Street so far downtown. I don't think it's healthy for you living in that box of a room and only drinking instant soup for food. And tea. Can't you move away? Even if you don't come to the mountains, can't you move away from Washington? There are other places in the world. How I wish you were free entirely of that heartbreaking city. If I could move this mountain, I would ask it to come to you and lift you and carry you away from Washington City. Do you remember Hains Point? And the kids playing with the statue there, *The Awakening*? His body buried, his arms and legs emerging, kicking, head thrust out horrified, trying to rise from underground. I have my own fears. What if we are never able to leave the mountains? Our race could die. A catastrophe could leave isolated pockets of black folk all over the Alleghenies without interconnection. I would be a pillar of salt trying to look back toward you. Our people could forget everything. Our race could die out completely.

Dear Johnnie, I feel that my soul is being threshed, and I am not well. Let me see you before I go. I love you so.

Your Grandmother Camille

# Sestren

HOLLOW ripples on the piano came through the open doorway. The walls around me were heavy, high, and dark with tapestries and saints, potted trees growing to the ceiling. The chair was a wooden throne and I stretched out my arms to hold the armrests. My feet just touched the floor. Trembling strong music. I held my head against the headboard and felt the velvet resilience. Appassionata. I had come exhausted from my Aunt Eva's to visit the convent and my Aunt Sister Cynthia Jane. I looked straight across at the marble feet of the holy saint as the music ended. I closed my eyes, winced, relaxed.

"Hello."

A surprising voice with a deep warm rumble within it. I looked up into her dark face, her dark eyes. Calmly she looked at me from the chancel entrance, her dark hands on the dark habit, waiting and watching. Yes, it is me, it is me at last. And it is you. I stood up.

"Sister Cynthia Jane?"

"Yes."

I've come, I've come to you. "I'm Johnnie." I've come. "My mother is gone and Diotima is gone and I ran from Georgetown to Aunt Eva on Logan Circle and now I've come to see you."

She walked up to me, two faces seeking each other, then she placed her hands on my shoulders softly. "Johnnie, so you've come at last?"

126

"Yes, I've come. I want to ask you about my mother. And about my father. Will you tell me where I've come from? Will you tell me who is my father?"

"Eva would not tell you? Nor your mother? Your father and our father are the same—John Christopher Snowdon. Dear Johnnie, you are born of father-daughter incest. It is a lonely and sad thing to know. Ah, may I hold you a moment? I know it's hard not to cry, Johnnie, but it's all right, here, hold on to me for a moment. You'll be all right. Come out into the cloister with me and let us talk together.

"Patricia used to tell me that her only clear image of herself was that of an empty skull. It's a puzzling image, a disembodied forsaken intellect. It has not been easy to reconcile that image with her passion, her passion not only for our father, John Christopher, but also her passion for Eva and for me. Soulless, disembodied, forsaken. But what is a soul?

"In nineteen sixty-nine, my great-aunt died, my mother's aunt, the one my mother had lived with since she was nine, the home she eloped from with our father, and before she died, she spoke about Patricia and said that Patricia was a child without a soul. She would feed on passion. She would inflict her emptiness upon all that has passion.

"Well, no one lives without a soul of course, but my great-aunt was referring to something in Patricia that we all recognized. The more I have thought of that image of the skull over these years the more it makes sense. The truth is that Patricia imagined herself with an unemotional intellect in order to avoid considering the moral choice she made in preferring sensuousness over goodness. It's not that she had an empty skull, but that she could not endure reconciling her choice of the senses over the mind and the soul. She chose to be soulless. My mother used to call her blasé. On her birthday or at Christmas Patricia would sit like a queen and comment on her gifts but she would never jump up and down with excitement for anything you gave her or about anything that happened—even if I was absolutely certain that she was filled with delight. She cultivated a separation between the parts of herself—mind, soul, emotions, body. And finally she chose to act out the body's desires—well, perhaps this is difficult to share, I'm sorry, often I think of these things to myself when I'm working over in the Senior Citizens' Home, I forget that I've not had a living audience for these thoughts before now, Johnnie. I spend three months of the year in silence—I often spin this story to myself.

"The Soul of Patricia. The Soul of the Daughter of the Father. I've come up with various titles of the story I tell myself about what happened. *Patricia*, you may know from the Latin, is derived from the word for *father, pater, patria, patrician*—father and nation. A name like that fits right into the myth she spun for herself and felt compelled to act out in her body...well, I hope you will accept from me this sharing of my thoughts so quickly. I suspect I will not see you again

127

after today. The order is thinking of moving to Indiana, since Washington is becoming uncomfortable with the rumors of war.

"Patricia interpreted everything mythologically in order to avoid focusing on the acts she was committing. She pretended to be classical—you know she studied all the classical languages—as a way of ignoring her passions, and the classics gave her an unemotional form for her passionate mythological self-portraits. There was such a strict disjunction between her intellect and her emotions—her lack of awareness of her interconnections freed her to act as if she repudiated the world, and her dramatization of this false repudiation was acted out as a mythological narration of incest and national identity—you see, *pater* and *patria*, father and country, as if somehow a new sphinx had asked the same old question, and she herself were the new answer.

"In any event my great-aunt's words affected us with a chill that was premonition. Eva believed it immediately. Dad left the room—it was the house out on Douglass Street—I suppose you have not been there, in the room that had been my mother's room before she ran away with John Christopher, right at the top of the stairs. My mother bent over her aunt and asked her not to repeat such things. But Patricia only laughed. That room had even been Patricia's room for a little while when my mother was in the hospital having Eva. My mother was quite ill when Eva was born. I stayed with Dad but my great-aunt kept Patricia— she was only two years old. My father and I would visit my great-aunt and my father would go upstairs and play with Patricia.

"Eva was sensual too, but not like Patricia. Eva was always falling apart psychologically when we were teenagers, forgetting herself, wandering the streets, not going to school. Some nights she crept into my room and clutched me. A few times she even tried to make love to me...but whenever she could she gazed at the curve of Patricia's body. Patricia was sensual but she never seemed to gaze at anyone then. I was in my second year of college, I've worked through the chronology so many times now, at Howard University in nineteen sixty-eight. That was the year a fire woke up in Patricia and it went for my father—ours.

"Is it too difficult for you to hear me? I hope it will not be so utterly upsetting. I've gone through it so many times and I've not spoken of it to my sisters here, yet I'm so used to thinking these thoughts, Johnnie, and who knows if I will see you again? She caught him everywhere in the house, smiling, kissing at him, playing with him as he turned and jerked away to his study, ashamed. We all heard. How he ran from her, and she kept after.

"And in the New Year, nineteen sixty-nine, in January, Patricia and Eva and I went to a meeting, a poetry reading on the Howard University campus. It was night and there was new snow on the ground. The three of us were to walk down and meet Dad in his office. But instead, after the reading, we stood out in the snow singing spirituals and mixing them up with some black street songs we had just learned. "Swing Low Sweet Chariot." "All of God's Children." "Mamma

128

Made a Bundle in the Bed." A strange combination really but we enjoyed it so much that night—we reminded one another of the three witches in *MacBeth*, truly we did, then Dad came and saw us, in that eerie light—can you believe there was actually a full moon? wild we sang, dancing, and he came up there and was somehow horrified to see us dancing together in the snow. We were so involved in the songs and making them interrelate I guess we seemed to exclude him. Certainly I felt the three of us were, or at least could be, very powerful that night. Ah, Daddy, Daddy, Daddy, what a bloody king he was walking through the snow to find us dancing there who will never dance together again, when, when, when shall we three meet again?

"That incident affected Daddy too much, I doubt that it would have meant so very much later if he had not tried to interrupt. He got it into his head that our singing and dancing together was somehow a way of hating life. No, it doesn't make much sense at all, he said we danced like that because of poetry that made us think we were superhuman—but we were only playing. And I suspect, Johnnie, it's more likely that he feared somehow that all three of us were lesbians. I've thought over these facts so long...of course we were not. We were three happy teenage girls in the process of growing up. Anyway he thought we would be cured by coming down to the hospital and watching him perform open heart surgery on a dog. He tried to show himself as a king and god. Eva and I didn't think much of the operation and didn't understand what he thought was gained in it, but Patricia was very much affected. She gazed at his fingers so, I remember it well, and when she held the dog's heart in her hands she called it the multifoliate rose. Dad didn't take Patricia's interest in him seriously, it seemed to me, until after the surgery on the dog.

"Patricia went after Dad and in March she caught him in his study and felt him all over his body, screaming at him as he tried to break away from her, she wanted so much to possess his body. Eva and my mother both heard them. Eva was standing outside Dad's study when it happened and then ran back to her room so they wouldn't find her there. She heard Patricia yell at him and refusing to let him go. As Eva was running back to her room she ran into my mother in the upper hallway—dazed, Eva told me, just standing there dazed and hearing and refusing to hear. My mother doesn't remember it, but I remember what Eva told me.

"Dad thought he could help Patricia recover from her passion for him but he was changing and falling in love with her. He thought he was helping, he thought by not running so violently from her he could help, but he made things worse. He started taking her out with him. He began to go out alone with her, letting her ride in the car whenever he returned to the hospital on patient emergencies. One morning there in January after they left the hospital they went downtown to the Mall. There between the Monument and the Reflecting Pool she lay on the cold ground and begged him to make love to her, that's what she told me after Eva came home from the hospital, she begged him to make love to her. He did not, but she told me that he almost did.

"A few days after that Patricia moved from the house to an apartment on Kalorama Road, hoping to make it easier to get him that way, giving him a place to come to so they could sleep together. He helped her to move and paid for it, thinking he was safer with her out of the house. He would go by in the car and pick her up and take her driving with him but still he wouldn't sleep with her. He would give her some of his office clerical work to do, but actually he was falling in love with her. His surgical magic failed. For the first time in his life his open heart surgery patients died right on the table—before that they had always survived the operation—and in mid-March, a young boy from the islands—I'm sure he secretly imagined him as his son, Dad pretended to us that he didn't care that he didn't have a son but I'm convinced that's what he wanted—this young boy he had worked over so hard, stitching and restitching his heart, began to die. He fought every day to keep him alive. He made up magic ointments and strange drips into his veins, holding life in the little boy against fate. He sweated and cried for the child's life. But when he left the hospital in the early dark mornings, Patricia was beside him. She actually told me later that she wanted to be his...I'm sorry, Johnnie, I keep forgetting that I'm talking out loud. Will you allow me to say it? She told me she wanted to be his bitch. That's the word she used, yes, I know it is hard, it's very hard. This is what I mean about her choice of being sensual rather than moral. It's a decision she made.

"At home we were mostly alone and waiting, my mother and I. Eva had been seeing a psychiatrist for quite a while by then. She never came home at all anymore and we were all too self-absorbed to go after her and bring her home. Sometimes she would come up to see me for an hour or so but she didn't seem to like the house at all once Patricia had moved out. But she would visit to let me know where she was. She was in a commune then, in a dark smelly room where I visited her once or twice. Why didn't any of us act to stop what was going to happen? The refusal of the human eyes to see what they must see is enormous. I can think of no acceptable excuses. I sat in my room writing poetry. My mother worked in the garden and was debating whether or not to go to American University to become a science teacher—she loved botany and geology—any natural science without blood it seems! We never saw Patricia in those days. Dad was in the house an hour or maybe two of twenty-four. His presence held the young boy alive. Every time he came home to rest they called him back to the hospital to try to save the boy.

"On April thirteenth my father fell asleep at the nurses' station at the hospital and the young boy died. Dad's heart was broken. He canceled all his other work for the rest of the month and packed his bags so he could go to San Juan to the child's funeral. The funeral was April seventeenth, nineteen sixty-nine.

"On April sixteenth, that night when Dad was already out of town, Eva walking late at night by the Old Carnegie Library, was raped. The police found her in the morning, her body exposed, naked, and bruised. They brought her raving to the psychiatric ward, Ward One, of Howard University Hospital, the old Freedmen's Hospital. My mother and I went to her. Dad as I said was already in San Juan. And where was Patricia? Somehow my mother and I both knew that morning as we went to the hospital, we were certain that she had gone to San Juan with Dad and that they had slept together the same night Eva was raped. Eva had somehow guessed it too and dramatized it that way so foolishly, with rape instead of with seduction, as it truly was. Patricia had gone to San Juan against Dad's will. She seduced him and rape had nothing to do with it. But Eva kept getting confused by those psychiatrists and she thought for a while that it had to be rape—ridiculous. Patricia was a...Patricia, that is, my sister, forgive me, Johnnie, but you know she was something of a whore.

"On April eighteenth Dad returned home but Patricia disappeared, afraid to let us see her. But the following week she returned to her apartment and went to visit Eva in the hospital. Eva finally woke up from all that disgusting Thorazine when Patricia came to her. And Eva forgave Patricia."

"Oh, Patricia, you are really here!"
"Yes. Sorry I couldn't make it with the others."
"I didn't know the others had been here."
"They've been coming every day for a week or so." Patricia sits on the edge of the bed and holds Eva's hands in her hands. "How are you, Eva?"
Eva smiled tenderly. "I'm fine."
"Are you then?" Patricia asks seriously, she isn't afraid like the others. "Outside you are broken, Eva, but how are you inside?"
"Really, Patricia, I'm quite well."
"I thought so. Are you going to let them cure you?"
"Somewhat, I suppose, I'm very weak..."
They moved closer together, hesitating...
"Talk to me, Patricia."
"What do you want, Eva?"
"What do *you* want, Patricia? You came here because you want something—I know you..."
"I want you not to hate me when everything is over. Don't look at me so harshly, Eva, you know I've had him, I'm going to have him more, there's no question."
"Patricia, are you so sure that's what you want from him?"
What I want? Of course it's what I want, it's a necessity."

131

"A necessity, Patricia? What did he do to you? What makes it so necessary? Have you thought about what made him do that with you—even though you did want it? It seems so strange, even cowardly not to examine—"

"You use hard words."

"You'll destroy our family if this keeps up—or maybe it's already destroyed and I can't bear to think it."

"It's not a question of destruction, it's a spiritual thing."

"Spiritual!? Patricia, it's a curse."

"I think you're wrong, Eva, you're not looking at it carefully enough. You can understand this, Eva, I'm sure you understand it already—I don't believe it comes from me, I believe it comes from God."

Their voices are calm in the long echoing hall of Ward One, poignant echoes touch the walls and fall coldly, penetrating. Patricia has the momentary poise of someone about to rise into frenzy, she is ready to move on to the next thing but lingers still over Eva's soft chubby almost-a-child's hands, trying to find a way...

"Would it have been worse for you"—and now their eyes meet—"would it have been worse for you if Dad had slept with you instead of me?"

Eva stares quietly into Patricia's face, stares and thinks and waits, her mind flinches stumbles and carries on obliterating an almost memory that thus loses its only chance to arise, she does not move. "No, Patricia, that wouldn't have been worse, I probably would have enjoyed sleeping with Daddy, but I don't know why."

Patricia relaxes. "Yes, I think so too but I didn't know if you knew it—or if you would admit it. And I bet you wouldn't be thinking about examining what made him do it either! I'm not afraid of sin and cowardice, Eva, I just want to sleep with my father, that's all I want to do, and I want one person to understand it. Will you take the time?"

Eva winces, trembles, and gives up. "It goes without saying, Patricia, that's what brought me here, I understand it but I don't know what it is I understand, and yet this is all I was thinking about as I walked and wandered downtown. And then I was raped!"

"You've spent a lot of time thinking about it already? So you are with me in this?"

"You don't know yourself very well, Patricia, it takes a toll to watch out for you—you don't care about anyone."

"I care about you and Dad and Janie."

"No, Patricia, you care about the image in your mind. Daddy and I, we have those images too—or visions—that make you feel closer to us, but you don't love us. As for Janie, you probably hate her." Eva calms the disturbance in Patricia's eyes. "Don't let it sadden you, I've already forgiven you and I suppose Daddy will too after a while, after he figures out what has happened when it's over. The others are lucky enough, they are not struck with these weird visions and

132

prophecies so they won't be broken, Ma and Janie will survive, they'll live on without us."

"Without us?"

"You take a toll."

"You think we're all going to die because of this?"

"No, but I think you will die because of it."

"Really? Is it as important as that?"

"I think so, Patricia—you know, I can't imagine the world without you, Daddy and I, I don't know how we're going to make it."

"I don't care about dying as long as I've got him."

"You'll have him *and* death—that's what I've been dreaming these days, but you know, you never really get him in my dream, or he never gets you. I don't know what happens. Where he was it was like heaven with gold and bright light glowing out of a carved metal street. He was happy to be there but you never looked at it or him. After you hounded him there somehow you forgot, you went the other way in space, but that's how you are. Think, Patricia, what are you going to do with him now? What's going to happen to him when he grows all in love with you? What are you going to do with him?"

"I don't care what happens then, I want everything to fall down."

"Johnnie, Johnnie, dear Johnnie forgive me, how I hated your mother in those days, I hated her and her lack of self-control and the inverted sickness she accentuated in our miserable lives, our sexually perverse family. I hate her." Janie's dark head drooped over the white surplice of the habit as she sat almost collapsed beside Johnnie in a corner of the cloister.

"I hate her, Eva, I hate Patricia." Janie is sunk in the chair. She tries not to fidget, tries to fake calm, blinking at the dusky red markings on the carpet.

Eva answers from her position on the bed. "And yet there is something so very appealing about her calm—and she is so very beautiful."

"All bitches have heats."

"I know you're right, and yet there seems to be something else that alters the meaning of what has happened. I guess I admire the clarity of her personal myth—and her persistence in achieving it. She feels no pain at all about what's happened, no guilt, no remorse, no second thoughts, nothing—I admire how empty she is of protest and pain."

"That fake!?"

"But she has a true falseness. Her falseness is her actual self. She's like zero made flesh—or that empty skull she keeps talking about."

"She's cold. She's conceited. I hate her."

"But no, it isn't hate—it's that she doesn't stand for anything, all that myth and yet truly it all seems so irrelevant when I talk to her."

"That's meaningless."

"How so?"

"How so!? How is it you can think so quietly about her? Hasn't she done enough to destroy us? Just look at this house! Look at this empty house of the damned! How could she sleep with him, our own father, how could she break him so when he was weak—she's stolen our father from us, she's stolen him, we're all bastards now! And you—what is it with you that every time somebody kicks you in the ass you sit back and admire their inner nature, their 'being.' Being! Bullshit! Why don't you just BE?"

"It seems to me that the easiest thing we can do with Patricia is dislike her— there must be something else—"

"And so just to be contrary—"

"No, not to be contrary. I keep telling you there is something else."

"What else? What else is there?" Janie wants to leap suddenly from the chair. She wants to pace and stop but she calms herself by sitting very still. Her dark black flesh hangs roundly on her cheeks. Her dark eyes focus on the nauseating white lacquer of a French table.

"She's so completely what she is. There's no doubt that she's complete."

"Completely what?"

"That's what I don't know. Innocent perhaps, that's what I keep wanting to say. Patricia is entirely innocent. But I don't understand where I get that from, I get so confused. I suppose she's completely evil. Maybe she's a complete fleshpoint of passion—the bitch like you said, a bitch in heat."

"And is our father the dog to cool her down?"

"No, I don't think so, I think he burns her and that he will keep burning her."

"So speaks Nero of Rome!"

"Janie, you shouldn't talk so harshly, it's not like you—does the culmination hurt so much then? Didn't you know it was coming?"

Janie jumps from the chair. "Bowwow, bowwow." She flings her arms up.

"Janie, please—"

"You know dog spelled backwards reads dog!?"

"Janie, you've got to get some peace in your mind—"

"And she doesn't even love him Eva, she doesn't love him, and he's beautiful."

"Be careful, Janie. Don't think about it until you can stand it. Find a way to stand it—"

"No, I will not, never. You're always making something reasonable out of something impossible. You can't step over a pile of shit without sticking a THINK sign in it."

"Piles of shit are extremely important."

"See what I mean?"

"Don't you believe that? I mean, I know you can't believe it all the time, but when you consider it, don't you believe important propositions can be hung on piles of shit? After all, shit is the by-product of the extraordinary act of converting light into flesh, the digestive system is an astounding furnace."

"What are you anyway, some kind of preacher? What do you mean 'Don't you believe...'? Is this some kind of religion? So I'm an atheist! Don't hand me no trash!"

"No, Janie, you know you're not an atheist. You're a Galahad in the midst of quest. You believe in goodness, you insist upon it. You're after the Holy Grail. You are the best among us, our genius—and you believe in divine love—I, I love Patricia because she's Patricia and I don't know how not to love her. But you are more true to God, and you are after a wholesome kind of love. And yet, is it ever confusing for you Janie, it's hard for me, do you ever think that even divine love may have some erotic love in it as well? I keep trying to understand how Daddy..."

Janie winced, struck out at air, broke into an almost cry yelling at Eva, "But love itself...love is the problem, Eva, love is forever getting in the way of achievement, blocking the access with pettiness, we can't live in peace, we can't die in peace because we imagine our beloved clothed in the perversions of love. Most of all we cannot complete the tasks we are ordained for, we deny God and fall into devils. It's wrong, Eva, it's wrong to see the world enclosed by our narrowness, why should Patricia feel justified in destroying the family with her passions? Why doesn't she care enough about us, about you and me, not to do it? Look at what is happening to us. You are becoming feebleminded, feebleminded. My mother a walking shadow and me so bitter and broken and my words won't come anymore. I have no free choices left, none at all. All I can do is try to preserve a fragment of myself, a sanity of fasts and meditations, which I pit against something else in me, even an insanity inside that rages against this house of the damned. Oh, Eva, do you think there is no vibrancy in me? Do you think Patricia is our father's only beautiful daughter? No, we were three—three powers, three goddesses or three witches dancing. We knew things when we were together. We understood the conjunctions of time and we were important together, we were a part of what was to happen.

"I was to have written it all down saying this happened and this happened, people would have understood, the world would have changed, Eva, under our impact and I had the words for it. I made the words to describe it, day and night a dream of articulation, a knowledge in me that whatever is can be spoken exactly and there is a word for everything. I believe it, Eva, I believe everything can be spoken and that I could have been the speaker. I was to have given a name to this age, Eva, but then this sick passion came out of Patricia's evil soul, or out of her empty skull as she would have it, pretty Pat, patPat, that's what he called her and the three of us just girls, babies, you and I, maybe you have forgotten it but I remember that the three of us held our arms in a circle happy and strong but he kept looking at her, I remember the way his eyes rested on her when she danced in the rain, squiggling her toes on the grass so happy and she was pretty when she danced there with her arms spread out in an X. I was fooled, I didn't think she was after him then, I thought she was dancing alone, yet he kept looking at her, forgiving her for her passion, calling her to him and he didn't even know it. I saw how he cared for her, kissing her beige skin until my blackness became a burden to me. It was all I could do to keep from crying. And he always touched her so softly, Eva, I remember when Ma was sick in the hospital and you were just about to be born and Patricia stayed down on Douglass Street, Dad and I would visit her and I remember how softly he touched her, once he yelled at me, Eva, so I wouldn't go upstairs anymore when he went up there to see her."

"I've lost something, Eva, I can't seem to pull my thoughts and my perceptions together anymore. She didn't have to do it, she didn't have to go after him, there was plenty of time and we cold have all been free. I can't forgive her, she had no business loving my father. She should have loved you and me. We could have done important things, something in me hates her now. I hate her. All day I walk in hate of her. My soul is hardened in me, I tell you the truth, Eva, my soul is a malediction, her passion stole my words from me, the words that were God's gift to me, for me to use to glorify my heavenly father but when she turns away from us and goes to him what can I do? I am empty. The words have an empty clang and they are not my words anymore. She perverts us. The hymns which were to go to God now go to some other creature, some enticing perversity spawned from those sinners, not God and not human, my miscarried poems.

"Oh, Eva, Eva, Eva, no more, it's too much crying, Eva why do you cry. Eva, Eva...

"There should not be love."

"We didn't see Patricia again until her birthday, June twenty-fourth, the day the great sinner was born, the destroyer of the family, and that was the last time we three met together. Neither thunder nor lightning nor rain nor even snow but bright summer sunshine. My mother insisted on giving Patricia a birthday party, although no one else wanted it."

My Aunt Sister Cynthia Jane sighed as she gathered her strength to continue with the story. She stood up from the bench and looked around nervously, glancing past my face beyond the columns of the cloister. Low under the trees the ferns curved and dipped. The moist warm breeze stirring heavy air, inaudibly space clicked into silence, the lovely Jesus face beside us drooped under its curls. "Divine Light," I thought to myself in that silence, "all is calm, all is bright." All was certainly still, as if the prayer-center had been invoked upon us. My thoughts frittered away as my Aunt Sister Cynthia Jane stood there—only, "This is the end of time," I thought, "now everything is over. This is forever at last."

"We are hearing the while. We have missed lunch, it is afternoon. This is when the sound of while comes, in the afternoon, that's what Patricia always said to me when she and I were little girls, taking naps together. How odd she was in the afternoons, she said she could hear while. She could hear the while and it would do strange things to her. She would sway and dance—especially in front of the window in the back room at our great-aunt's house—when the flecks of dust would move within the thin slats of light. She danced within those slices of light and I watched. But she was beautiful like that, swirling the dust like sprinkles of precious metals or flecks of transparent jewels. She would close her eyes just so, to make rainbows through her eyelashes when she lifted her face. And she would raise both hands high and wide above her head and stand with both feet apart just so in an X shape as in a dance, the lovely Patricia, how I loved her then, the little girl, my sister. I wanted to give her everything. I kept hoping there would be a way for me to do something so special for her, even to die in order to save her when I grew up. The lovely Patricia who loved only silence and emptiness and extinct beauty. If you had ever seen her in those moments, Johnnie, after raising her arms like that she would make this chilling gesture of pushing the air away from her, that false repudiation, if you had seen her you would know that she never loved anyone, not anyone human. patPat indeed, if she was a heartbeat, she was one emptying out until it was dry.

"She loved stillness and pure quiet. It was the desire for inarticulation that made her love languages so much, her words pieced out silence until they were all the rhythms of an absolute cosmic nothing. Patricia and silence. That silence in which she created passion." My Aunt Sister Cynthia Jane turned away from me, looking through the pine tree tips to the sky. "Perhaps Eva was right, Patricia was zero made flesh. Her intellect was the mind of nothing, the emptying skull— forgetting, contradicting, careless as a pagan god. She was so careless in passion, and passion itself was a form of nothing in her. She only wanted an excuse to sit and dream in Georgetown. She was all we turn away from in our struggle away from earth to the heaven of Jesus, the Christ. And so beautiful. I used to shudder when I saw her smile. Really, I used to shudder. Her smile changed all the rules.

"Yes, Johnnie, once there was a little girl who thought the dust-filled slats of light pouring through the window in the back room were gods. 'While,' she said to herself, amusing herself, 'While, while, while' playing, she said. 'While, while, while, while, while.' She danced in the afternoon, danced in the sun, danced in the dust of the sun, repeated a word. 'While' and 'while.' But the silence, seeping between her tongue and palate. 'While.' And then her head was light, the air blurred to quietness. 'Dust, bright dust, my cheek, my hair, dust, layers of light, floor to window, dust, washing upon me in light, breathing it, squinting.' And after quietness came silence and emptiness, that gesture of raising her arms then casting the air away in repudiation and after that Patricia fell asleep in the afternoon.

"She danced at her birthday party with the sun in the window, not a storm. The last time we were together, Dad, my mother, Patricia, Eva and me, all at once.

"Eva put the music on. I stooped before the coffee table arranging cookies and plates my mother had handed to me from the kitchen. Were we playing statues? Until Patricia stood and danced to the music. Eva standing at the window looking out at the sun. My mother's step upon the carpet with her focus just above Dad's head.

"Patricia stood up lightly and turned toward the high glass wall between us and the greenhouse, lifted her arms and danced. None of us moved until it was over. No one cried out loud but I thought how good it would be if we could lock the outside doors forever, and stay there, the five of us, alone with ourselves entirely forever, until our minds stopped beating.

"Dad tried to stay away from Patricia. Even though her seduction of him had been consummated he was managing not to let it happen again, trying to talk Patricia out of it and find her something to do. I think he was having a hard time keeping his concentration together in the lab but he would still give her assignments relating to the office, trying to keep her mind occupied, but he didn't share his struggles with my mother or anyone, as far as I know. He struggled by himself all day in the hospital and he would struggle alone at night sitting there in the chair. I think he wanted to be with Patricia yet he held himself with us, he sat in the living room staring out the window or into the rug.

"How the world seduces us after all. That was a beautiful summer and autumn for me in spite of the family horror. I took long walks near the park, and long baths, and I would day-dream for hours, thinking poetry. Wondering what would happen next. The house filled up with passion. It filled all the air. It was in the walls and windows. It trembled when I touched the ledge or when I sank back into a pillow. It was with my mother in the greenhouse, in the warm heat of the flowers and leaves. It hovered above my father, who was almost blurred with it as he passed through the rooms. Sometimes the room swirled violently around him and I would have to shut my eyes and go away. I cried many evenings. The sort of cry that is a part of pleasure, a sinful pleasure in love's sorrow.

"Eva wouldn't stay at home after recovering from the rape—she went back downtown. She mailed postcards to me, but they were just short descriptions of her strange dreams. She was calling herself a prophet. She had taken the green crystal ball that Dad had given her, and she carried it around the streets with her, making up prophecies and stories, getting into trouble. Sleeping with tramps, lesbians, living in bars. It sounded very miserable.

"During these same days Patricia was gathering her strength to get him back, to make Dad lose his power and want her, and to come to her whenever he wanted her, whenever he needed her body and to have no barrier between the sickness of the desire and the sin of the act. In that very perfect September, she

138

told me that she had almost given up and was actually looking over her language books debating working on that when she finally succeeded with Dad. He visited her in the apartment when she was looking over her languages for a change, he took her from her apartment and drove her through Rock Creek Park. They pulled to the side of the road where he gave himself up again this time without the excuse of the dead boy. He reached under her dress and played with her. He reached, he touched under her blouse and trembled. That was all for then. He recovered in a moment and took her back to her apartment, but then a few days later he went by and found her truly working with her languages, Mandarin and Russian and Portuguese and all the others she loved so much. He saw her working there without him, absorbed with what she was knowing and forgetful of him in spite of all her proclaimed passion and joy for him. She was in the small study room of her apartment and they had agreed long before that if ever she should be working there he would not come in. He saw her there only a few days after the park incident when she had lured him, whimpering for him.

"He dragged her out of her study and into the bedroom and he made love to her all night. All night for many other nights thereafter.

"Patricia started her first year at Howard University that semester. She was taking a class in Greek, ancient Greek, among other things. The professor in that class helped Patricia a little. She didn't know what was wrong with Patricia, but she figured out that she wasn't capable of following regular study. The professor thought Patricia would progress more quickly with individual study and suggested that Patricia leave the university and contact a special tutor to help her concentrate on her work. She gave Patricia the address of her Mexican friends, the Mexican professor of Greek and his daughter, Diotima. Diotima lived out in Eastland Gardens and helped Patricia to find another place to live when Dad tried to stay away from Patricia and make her get a job and find something to do—he wouldn't pay for the apartment anymore. I don't know all the details of how the relationship grew between Patricia and Diotima, but that autumn they began to meet each other. Patricia evidently knew that some end to this incestuous relationship was coming. Dad was falling too quickly. His work was going to hell. Patricia knew that Dad would never let his work fall entirely into hell and that an end would come.

"Also, she herself, although she pretended to want Dad had times when she didn't want him at all. She still kept having those blank moments when nothing made any difference, including Dad and her fantastical foreign words. We talked a long time about it. She told me that while he was with her in bed she would sometimes forget what she was doing and would just be staring at a Renoir, *By the Sea*, that she had on the wall.

"Passion kept changing into indifference like the swan in Yeats' poem. But then she was both the swan and Leda, and my father was both of them too. They

139

mingled so much with each other, it was hard to tell who was the possessor and who was the possessed.

"And she still believed in her myths, she actually quoted Lot's daughters to me, 'Come, let us make our father drink wine, and we will lie with him, that we may preserve seed of our father,' as if we lived at the end of the world.

"Patricia, why won't you have mercy on him?"

"Mercy, Janie, what is mercy? He's beautiful, the most beautiful lover in the world. Do you think I could see him and not try to take him? You know he's beautiful. Don't you know he's beautiful?"

"How can you call him beautiful now when he's weak and miserable and angry with you for seducing him?"

"I like him angry. I enjoy the heat that leaps from him when he yells at me, when he breaks against me, screaming and pleading for his life. He has my life too. He has had my life. And I'll have him. Ha-ha, sometimes I wonder at the sweetness of it, Janie, how I enjoy his heat, his heavy fire falling on me."

"Why can't you find someone else to satisfy you? Why can't you leave him alone?"

"Why? Janie don't you know he's my only possible companion in the world? And I want him in me when I need him there. The best lover—you know, Janie, they say somebody else's husband makes the best lover—I've just picked the most convenient adulterer around, Janie, he does it good, floats me like a cloud."

"Oh, Patricia, I wish you wouldn't talk about it like that! It's awful. I don't like to hear about it."

"Ha-ha, it's not awful, Janie. It's warm and brown like pumpernickel you know, ha-ha, the bread that can feed the five thousand and then some, the bread that can be broken and still rise to feed again, and let it rise, Janie, let it rise again and again and fill me up, may it come to me pompous, strange, trembling, long awaited—oh, can't you understand that without this there would be nothing? Can't you see how this is more important than everything, how seldom within the world are we given to each other, to be transported beyond desire into the heart of god, with fire and terror and awe—it's a gift, it's a gift from god that cannot be refused and I will have god, I will have god within me for all time forever eternally completely absolute—I will have god and only god as my lover."

"God? Patricia, are you calling our father God? Daddy is not God, God is God, God is a spirit."

"I'm not talking about Dad specifically, Janie, you don't understand at all. You're damn right Daddy is not the spirit—but the god who is spirit is easy to come by, that god, that god is everywhere, I've known that god all my life, the sexless god of everything. That's easy, that's too damn easy. I've already stood at the top of heaven, Janie, I've already looked god face-to-face. It bores me, the eternity of god is trite and dull and so painfully easy—it's enough to make me cry—to walk with god all the days of my life, I've had enough of it—but what's hard? What's the only thing that's hard in the whole damn world? What is hard, Janie, is to get your body laid, to be somebody's bitch. If I were a heaven I would break myself. I would be Satana and carry with me my third part of heaven. Eternity is long to have only your mind and nothing else..."

"What are you talking about, Patricia? This is ridiculous. We're talking about you and Daddy and incest—and you are a female and Daddy is a male and I don't believe God has a thing to do with it..."

"Don't you, Janie? So much the worse for you. But take your curses somewhere else, I don't need you—"

"Do you love him, Patricia? Just tell if you love him. I didn't come over here just to fight with you. Will you tell me if you love him?"

"Love, Janie?" And Patricia's voice broke and trembled, slowing. "He asks me the same thing. When I'm away from him I think of him—or I can write words sometimes, but I really have to work at it—it doesn't come naturally to me. It seems bigger than love to me, love is a small word, it doesn't hold enough, it's too human—"

"But you were just saying how earthly things are more desirable than heavenly...and if you consider love human..."

"Janie, how can you understand? Passion and sex, that passes so quickly. It can excite me for a moment, but I know better. Eternity is inescapable and takes me with it. Even though I should speak all the languages of the world and should stand before the face of the last emptiness and speak every word in the world, one word at a time, and whole ages were given for the repeating of those words, still at the end would no thing come forth, and the emptiness which is forever would sink back on itself and I would be where I have always been from the very beginning. It's so sad. Life would have been such a beautiful idea, but there has never been life, nothing has ever been created, there is no creation, and there has never been a live thing in the history of the world."

"I think you are crazy! I think you've lost your mind."

"If I am it's because you will not hear me. Your mind is greater than any I know and if you can't understand then I cannot be understood and I'm right in believing there's no place for me on earth."

"There's no room for incest and sloppy immoral thinking. There's no room for—"

"Do you love me, Cynthia Jane, do you love me?"

"What?"

"Do you love me?"

"No, Patricia. No. I won't be like they are with you, I won't forget what you do because you dazzle people and make us forget, I won't let you do it to me, no, I don't love you, I cannot love you."

141

"You should have found a way to love me, my sister, maybe I would have found a way to live if you loved me. You didn't even love me before Daddy. You always liked the joy I bring but you think I am foolish. You don't like me. Ah, Janie, many times I would have been linked with you. Genius you are, great in truth, but you are like the vacant god I move toward, you smile and turn away. You smile and turn away more than I ever turned from life into emptiness. I've never had enough of the world—life piled on life would be all too little."

"Patricia, Pat..."

"One life after another, Janie, my sister"

"Please no more, Patricia—now—"

"Held in Eva's arms. Has she not held us, you and I, both, as you and I recoiled with burns from each other?"

"Yes, yes, Eva..."

"And maybe this is really what's happening here, Janie, a lesser of evils, I am unable not to long for the light that is yours, but I cannot be you or be with you without dirtying you—I choose rather to damn myself and our father than to soil your greater—"

"No Patricia, please..."

"I love you. Hear it now so you know. With you there is no hesitation. I speak to you what I can speak to no one else. I love you, and I ask you to remember this hereafter."

"Pat, Patricia."

"Cynthia Jane."

"Good-bye."

"And I never saw her again, Johnnie. I never saw her again." And there, in the late afternoon sunshine, before the altar, Janie cried, laying her head on my lap. She cried.

"Soon after that you were conceived. February nineteen seventy. I stopped attending classes at Howard—I was going over to the National Shrine to pray every day, praying for the forgiveness of our family. It seemed then that everything happened because of the failure of love on my part. If I could have found a way to understand the way Patricia was—but I never did.

"Eva came back from the commune in March. She dreamed that you were conceived. I don't think Eva was ever crazy. Patricia was insane but Eva never was. Eva's problem was even more complicated. She was too pure in her feelings. She loved too much, she was full of love, and she would take so much time to hold Patricia and I to each other. Sometimes—during the earlier years—if Patricia and I were reading in different parts of the house, Eva would come and take me by the hand and lead me to where Patricia was—or she would take Patricia and bring her to me—and she would insist that the three of us sit and read together.

"Once the three of us took a class together—a seminar on modern British poetry given down at Smithsonian's—what a class that was! The poetry seemed to go all inside of Eva, and Patricia and I were so embarrassed sitting on either side of her. Sometimes she would sit there playing with my hand and in spite of myself I would—I would be embarrassed and ashamed at the feeling—you see she would always surprise such feelings out of me.

"It was natural for Eva to feel and touch people and things. She felt the fluid things. Once during that class I had to take a pencil out of her hands—she was just playing with it, you know, in her fingers, looking up at the teacher, and I swear, looking at how she touched that pencil, everybody in the room broke into a fever! The teacher was blushing awfully but he couldn't look away from her—we were discussing Gerard Manley Hopkins I remember. It was awful. And I took the pencil out of her hand so he could finish talking. And she was so young to bring out such reactions.

"She brought out the same feelings in Patricia, Patricia and I talked about it, and even though she could stand it more than I, Patricia thought it was awful too. We were wrong. Patricia and I were wrong—Eva was so pure and natural we decided she was perverse. Patricia and I disagreed on morality, but at least Patricia knew the difference between perversion and normal behavior according to how the world thinks. Eva never knew. Eva touched people because she loved them, or because they looked good to touch and touch was so good to her. She would touch a desk and the wood of it would begin to remember where it came from, how it had pulled its sap from the mud up to the leaf—and a blade of grass twined in her fingers—we knew how the small transparent cells opened themselves for her touch. Her touch was promiscuous—a promiscuous love-body moving from dream to dream. Polymorphous pervert, we called her, virgin-whore. She never thought it was perverse to touch her sisters as she did, shame for that was never in her.

"Poor Eva, she wore herself out trying to hold the family together. It was her habit to catch us all up by the hand and bring us to one another—but that's what caused the problems. We were such an insular family to begin with that whenever anyone of us approached another too closely, the relationship changed into incest. Eva's habit of always bringing us together emphasized all this. This is what she wanted to escape when she went downtown. It wasn't so much being a prophet—though she did take the trappings of that, it was an attempt to escape the perpetual sense that we were hovering on the verge of incest in all our dealings with one another. She finally realized and believed how much we were unlike her. We couldn't touch and remain pure. She saw the despair we were racing to as a family, and she saw herself as the catalyst, the innocent catalyst.

"Seeing the estrangement at Patricia's birthday party, noticing our father's downcast face as he looked away from Patricia's erotic dance, she made up her mind to leave.

143

"Eva's sin was innocence and unconsciousness. It's funny how we were always accusing one another of representing various forms of nothingness. Patricia found me incapable of love and normal human responses and yet who has ever been more empty than Patricia? Eva had her blankness too. If, as she played in public with our hands and fingers, she never noticed the strange looks we received, it was because she was somewhere else in her mind. She wasn't there with us at all, she was asleep. And if she was asleep with us she was awake somewhere else, but what could I know about the blankness between where she stood with us and where she lived with her mind. How could we find out about that—twisting as we did toward and away from one another, braiding in and out of one another like plaited trinity.

"We were an awful trinity, Johnnie, and sometimes even now I start to my feet from prayer, afraid. Seriously afraid. Ah, let me not pray to the wrong God. I can tell you, Johnnie, I've paced my way toward God with all faith and joy and expectation but nevertheless, there are moments I start to my feet praying forgiveness so fervent my body will not kneel but must race here in the trees pleading—or I go to music—we all went to music, the three of us. I would play and Patricia would dance and Eva would sing and the song would be the song would...I can't...I can't speak of it...the song cannot be spoken.

"This is how we destroyed our father. Eva stirred us so into touch that should not touch and that class at Smithsonian's brought it all to a head and the poetry workshop at Howard was soon after that when we were all filled up again and Daddy saw us there in the snow the trinity of nothingness crying out the song of its self-sufficient vacancy and Daddy saw us, my God, sometimes even I am caught up in their mythologies. Johnnie, you must not believe them. Patricia kept saying that she was the sign of the fall of Washington, that her empty skull was the Capitol dome, and finally that you, her child, would restore the soul of the city, that you would be the light in the skull—all false mythologies, Johnnie, do not believe them. Believe only in the one true God and forget this other. Think through it, yes, because you must, but don't overthink the time. Forget what I have told you when it is time to forget...

"We all found out that Patricia was pregnant, my father, my mother, and I— and we all knew how by whom and Dad begged her to get an abortion, he tried to force her to get an abortion but I was already thinking I would become a nun and I couldn't recommend abortion and Eva went to Patricia and told her to be sure to have the baby but Dad was going to give Patricia the abortion himself, he went to her apartment with all the medical stuff and everything but Patricia cursed and cried and took a butcher knife to him swearing she was having the baby and he ran like a scared puppy all the way from her apartment to Sixteenth Street, he went running all the way home to my mother.

"But before he got home he almost had a heart attack, he had to pullover to the side of the road because of chest pains and his hand and arm stiffened up and

144

he knew he was going to die. He thought he was going to die. He hightailed it home with his heart leaping out of one side but he made it back to my mother.

"It was her moment. My mother. For that moment she had waited. She rested her husband. My mother went to Patricia, to comfort her. She gave her money and comfort and sent her away to have you in peace. Diotima got a room for Patricia secretly at the Heights Community Center, where Dad couldn't find her.

"In June I came here to the convent, yes, and went into my first long period of silence here. As for our family, I called it Egypt and left it. I don't communicate with any of them. Patricia sent some of her letters and papers to me here to be kept in the motherhouse vault. I've actually brought this packet for you, it's just a small portfolio of a few of your mother's letters. Maybe you'll want to read them over on your way to visit your grandparents this afternoon. I must go now, Johnnie. I'm going back into silence and I doubt that I will see you again. Resist evil, try to resist it in spite of everything.

"And you? On November eleventh, nineteen seventy, I was handed a letter from Patricia telling me you were born on November third."

# My Grandparents' Door

I felt out of breath as soon as I stepped off the bus at Sixteenth Street and Colorado Avenue. I didn't see a yellow plaster house. I could see between the houses to other clumps of houses that were facing another street, but they were all of gray stone.

The house directly in front of me had a NO TRESPASSING sign in the large triangular yard. Yellow brick with yellow brick columns and a black roof. There was a round sign between the two middle columns, with a small sailboat on a blue and red background, but the words were too small to read. Footsteps came toward me. She was a lively brown wife talking and gesturing and he was an orange husband who was laughing and trying to find a break to answer back. They smiled and passed on either side of me.

A yellow plaster house. The only yellow plaster house on the block they told me. The sky was a perfectly clear blue mid-morning springtime sky. On the other side of the street there were tall full trees set back on the grass. Rock Creek Park Carter Barron Amphitheater. On my side of the street the sidewalk and curb were dark gray stone separated by a strip of striking green grass measured out with trees. The leaves glistened.

The student I bumped into continued her conversation with two other students while glancing at me. The words she directed to them hit against my face. She had a broad face and full blue eyes and white skin and her cheeks stood out from her face and her lips were small and moving, and her forehead was

146

deep, her curly blond brown hair combed back from her face. Leonine. Her eyebrows were light brown. The second student had her long brown hair tied in a cord, and the third student had brown skin and short nappy hair and a purple jacket. I didn't answer anything. They passed behind me and I continued up Sixteenth Street.

A gray stone house with four large windows across the top story. A red roof with a gable. Across the street at the edge of Rock Creek Park, tennis courts.

Another gray stone house facing the tennis courts, four large windows, red roof with a gable, and a sign reading DR. FALMAN. The sunlight poured down between the houses and trees. Eye-stinging shafts of light. A red brick house with a gray roof and three windows. A little boy skipped by in front of a teenager in a plaid skirt. They both wore bright red scarves. A yellow stone house with a red roof and three gables facing across to a soccer field. Across the street the tennis courts had changed into a soccer field. Far behind the field a forest was bending closer to Sixteenth Street.

A house that is a church. Iglesia Evangelica Menonita Hispanica and a solitary lady with a cross around her neck and a book under her arm walking down the steps nearest the curb. A blue leather skirt and vest with a blue and pink and white flowered blouse gold brown hair and a book under her arm staring straight ahead. The white plaster church was smooth and the top-floor windows were open and curtains were hanging outside. Green figures along the border on a white background. I couldn't see what the figures were. Above the windows the sun slanted against the black roof and hit me full in the face. The lady got into a glowing yellow car with a yapping beagle while another loud car, blasting saxophone music, roared around her. A family. A husband. A wife. Two little boys. A dog. Music.

And finally there was a yellow plaster house, but it had strips of wood set into it. That couldn't be the place. The house was set far back in the yard—the yard had a red stone fountain of bubbling water filling up a small circular basin of stone. The trees around the edge were extremely high and formed a complete canopy but the grass around the fountain was ragged and dead and the bushes around the edges of the garden were ragged and unkempt. Because the house was set so far back from the street there was a stark patch of sunlight on the red roof burning at the back of shadowy trees. I wanted to go in.

A yellow brick house so tall and unsloping that I could barely see the roof from where I stood on the sidewalk. Five very tall windows across the top story. I stretched my neck and could just see that it had a red roof but the glare and the stretching made my eyes hurt.

A house entirely of yellow plaster. This should be it. It looks almost mystically religious with three immense arched windows, two stories high, the largest one in the center flanked by two smaller ones, all engraved with delicate pale gold lotus flowers. And a roof of real curved Spanish tiles, not shingles but bright red tiles, and the oddest most exotic yellow chimney rising from it I had ever seen. I immediately decided it was Moorish, since I had no idea what a Moorish chimney would look like, with intricate grates and curves and loops. What a wonderful marvelous chimney! What must they cook in this house to need such a chimney! I walked through the neat hedges and up to the door. It was partly open. I touched it and it opened completely. A Krishna worshipper stood there in the dark with light on her hair blinking reciting something, "transparent like a pure crystal," she said while her hair glistened. The light poured around me through the door. How I wanted to stay there, but it wasn't my grandparents' house after all.

As I stepped back down through the hedges I noticed that on the other side of Sixteenth Street the soccer field had become a baseball field. A gray sidewalk divided the fields. Along the edge of the baseball field there were benches and tables set up under a few of the trees for talking and lunch. Behind the baseball field the forest of Rock Creek Park swept closer.

A house of red brick and wood, more modern than the others with a sign, AFRICAN SISTER, in red and black and green. Gigantic block letters were stretched across the next house, Chù Ciác Hoàng, with a hundred tall flags waving in a row behind the windows BUDDHIST CONGREGATIONAL CHURCH OF AMERICA and a smaller note on the door, "Indra's Bow."

Three gables in a red roof above four windows in a yellow brick house. A Mexican walked toward me in a white suit with the jacket open and a roll of papers under his arm. He had a large square face with a square chin with a little dent under his lip and a moustache under his straight nose and deep-set brown eyes with soft folds in the corners and thick arched brown eyebrows and a high forehead and curly brown hair and he was looking at something inside his head and the pastel orange shirt underneath the white jacket had decorative little holes in it and no tie so that I could see his chest through the holes and he almost ran over me because I didn't move out of the way but at the last minute he swerved around me on my left without looking at me.

Then I finally came to the Snowdon family house for the first time. It was a Spanish-style house in yellow plaster. With arches connecting four square columns. A Spanish tile roof. A greenhouse bending around the corner from the back. I was nervous.

Halfway up the path I stopped and looked around. There was a huge church next to the house. Sixth Presbyterian Church for Koreans in Washington, D.C. Beyond the church was the street that ran directly into Rock Creek Park. Kennedy Street. The forest bent away down a hill.

I looked up at the door. I was afraid. I walked up to the door. I looked the door in the face. I lifted my hand and knocked. This was it.

The door had a small window and a thin lace curtain. I could see into a long living room and then my grandmother Camille's face on the other side. She

opened the door to me. I stood there. We faced each other. "Good afternoon."
"Good afternoon. Are you Mz. Camille Snowdon?"

"Yes...but your eyes, your...but who?"

"My eyes? You recognize them? My mother told me that they are like yours."

Johnnie

# Pianoforte

CAMILLE, staring into the blotted page of music, touching her fingers against ivory keys, waiting for John Christopher to come to marry her

Camille

The day is so hot, so bright, so full, the air is so full of light she trills a few notes that push through the moist heat then with both hands the first of Bach's three-part inventions the first notes but her left hand stumbles.

"Dear God, please make him come for me today."

Her left hand drops on the bass keys, hits between two wrong notes, her hand falls downward farther misses the keys, fingernail scratches the wood the damp palm of her hand then the scratch on the grain of the wood

And again

Lifts her hands to the music. Baroque clarity, rapidity, abundance, in Kenilworth on Douglass Street, her hands on the keys break cool music into hot humid air.

She moves from the music her mind withdraws from the page and she turns toward the window—the lilac bush leaves are dark and thick, the grass neat and precise. The grass has not grown between the cracks of the sidewalk; does not straggle on the footpaths.

"What if a dust storm flattens all the corn in the garden and I were to stand here tired wondering how I would ever have red tomatoes again with no rain and

150

there have been so many days I sat in the heat and ate those tomatoes I want him to come for me now?

"What if nothing happens?"

Restlessly she places her hands on either side of the bench and bends her upper body toward the window at her right. She hooks her feet between the piano pedals and the thick rug. Her legs and abdomen are a soft curve beginning at the waist, but above she distorts toward the window, squints in reaction to the light that burns on the dark leaves of the lilac bush, gone wild.

"Yet he may not come for me although my nightgown is already packed, fluffed, tucked sheer blue, white lace, puffed sleeves, silk bows, streaked with light, light shining and filtering through a dusty room.

"When I put it on the hem rests between my knees and waist, my legs curve down from it, I am embarrassed to see myself I wonder if he will like the way my legs curve down from my nightgown I wonder if I am beautiful I wonder if he will hold me quickly and love me or if I must wait and wait I wonder how much he'll want me I wonder if he will want me very much and I wonder if he is even going to come at all today to get me because I'm waiting for him to come all day upstairs and downstairs waiting, not sleeping, not anything but arranging my perfumes, fiddling with my powders all in the same scent I have talcum and bath oil and perfume and lotion and cologne and I'll put them on my body and he will love me, I've just been playing this piano."

White lace on blue silk, crocheted by hand, and the sheer blue gathered between the rows of lace perfectly, sweetly, "I wonder if I'll even put it on at all but if he doesn't come what good is a train case filled with perfumes and powders?" her eyes on the notes her fingers on the keys perspiring "I won't stop now I won't wipe my hands yet but I will keep playing the song until I can play it."

It is hard work for her keeping busy all morning, all afternoon, upstairs and down, upstairs she lies across the white cotton bedspread and sheets, it is so hot and she lies there perspiring and weak, wishing wanting to push time. She doesn't want to look out of the window because the sun moves too slowly, the light is always the same light, it is always the same place in the sky, it is hard work for her thinking of something to do.

"For a while I hated the dog next door. I grit my teeth and cursed at his barking 'Shut up you damn dog.' I cursed him under my breath. I tried hating the dog in the yard under my window because it gave me something to do. 'Damn you stupid dog.' And there wasn't anything to bark at anyway, 'Damn damn dog!' But after a while he stopped barking and morning was only half gone and I was too restless to stay upstairs so I came downstairs but there was nothing to do and so I went back upstairs.

"And I felt a creeping outside of me that wanted to come inside, a tugging at the hair on my arms but it was nothing and I sat in the chair waiting, I sat without any music I sat without moving I sat trying to be good enough for him to come for me if I pray hard enough if I think hard enough maybe...but the air was heavy dropping around me the heat grew hotter but the day stood still there was a glow from the rug, the rug was woven melted kernels of fire and there was no escaping it, it came after me it crept across the floor, the heat, it flattened the wool nap, it lifted its waves to brush the hair on my arms it wanted me to come."

Dozed or dazed in the chair

Camille

She sows a green garden in her mind

Camille melted and softened by heat, draped in moisture, blinded by warm and wet the heat went after her the heat blurred the windows, waxed the floor the heat wilted her mind, smudged her face half in sleep, covered her, peered deep— strained at her pores, and Camille's body wept

She sows a green garden in her mind

And a loud whine from the playground down the street roused her and she came down to her piano.

"What if a dust storm were to flatten the corn? What if the pictures of the fields were blotted out speck after speck while I tried to sleep restlessly but the dog still won't stop barking no matter how long I wait and how could I sleep today of all days so I came downstairs to play the piano instead is he going to come, is he?"

Downstairs, she grasps for the song she clenches it breathes relaxing she batters into the song then breaks she holds plays herself away, somewhere else someplace like the lily ponds in Kenilworth where once Chris couldn't help it but when she stood on the cement bridge lord how he pulled her down from there and his arms around her legs and his hand almost up against her thighs between her thighs and he pulled her and kissed her and kept kissing her while his arm pressed the back of her legs pressing her until she felt how hard he was and she was happy and kissed him back but her dress had come up when she finally whimpered and wanted him to make love to her right then, right then he stopped

Camille

In her mind a green garden

Remembers the redbrown of his face, the dark transparent outer skin, a film over the red undercolor of his face. The brown skin holding his blood, the brown skin keeps him inside

Camille

A green garden

Broke and broke at the music

He is coming for her, he is coming right now in a smile in a car, he will take her somewhere he will take her yes he will drive up and she will see him from the porch and though she has been waiting so long though she has been thinking maybe he will come maybe he won't she will smile up on the porch when he

152

comes at last to take her the music scatters. She melts, disintegrates between lines within open circles looped in the white spaces held within the musical signs— each note plucked from the page and flicked into the white hot air by the quirk of her eye.

And the song stands still again. Then with the left hand alone she comes back striking the keys creeping timidly then clearly, slowly making her way through the lower notes. An animal's multi-feet pressing against smooth slats, her fingers inch out the music note by note, a desert animal's feet brushing against white hardened sand glazed bone her fingers advance along the white keys.

He came once, he brought yes flowers and took her to his apartment where he started by kissing her cheek and she was all the time immediately in love with him and they played a game of Monopoly and she ended by laying herself down on him so gently he sweetened her she skips and plays along the music again and again pouring and sparkling back again she dances the lilt of the song her hand finds the chords and scatters them, places them brightly upon the walls.

It improves. If she can only hold her hand just so, just so, and love the keys as she plays the left hand only. And she plays the left hand not because she cannot play both but because of the special love she has for it, it is hers it plunks like she plunks the left hand notes are like Camille

In her mind she sows a green garden

She dreams a green garden and in that garden a butterfly lifting from the cocoon in blue orange cruising above the flowers extravagant (what shall I do with you) brushing against the tips of the grass (o lord) no higher than that the left hand song moves clearly, the left sweet song

Gently he had sweetened her gently she was sweetened

"If I leave here today I will not come back tonight, it is a long way to be married.

"But my aunt will wonder where I am, she will look for me on the porch and in the garden, I won't be in my room and she will wonder where I am she'll have dinner for two but I won't be here and I'm not coming back.

"She takes care of me. She buys me pretty dresses she doesn't let me work too hard she wants me to stay home she wants me to buy a fish box every Saturday night and bring it home to eat with her she wants me to lock boyfriends on the other side of the screen door she wants me to turn my back on them and come to her.

"I want Chris."

"She wants me to always have a dime to call home with and a token to ride home with and cab fare just in case, in case something happens when I'm out and I need to get home she wants me to kick them when they touch me, if they touch me, whenthey iftheywantme, their minds are only on one thing they all want to get me back in a corner she wants me to spit in their faces.

"I want Chris I want him to come for me now."

153

He came once and again and again and again and she loved him all the times he came he was coming to marry her today she walked through the song it was easy he was coming to make her his wife

Camille

Green eyes, tan orange skin, she lowered her head blushing downward whenever he came

Camille

Thin lips, thin waist, thin legs, thin sandy hair curled on her shoulder

Camille

She is the one he comes for, she is the one who sows a green garden in her mind while seated at the piano waiting for him to come. The music.

She is the most beautiful of all. Sitting on a hill once she sat and looked out over the reservoir at Howard University when the air was dusky and filled with the talk of students, sound bulged doors and windows, sound was a batter of thick soup she sat there. She tried to ignore the beauty turned away from reflection and sunset looking away from the water. Beauty bombards her. She opens her eyes to cool wind and the light of sunset on glassy water pierced, she is more beautiful than anyone this is how Chris saw her first and she is the only one Chris comes for

Camille, she is the queen

The music she plays is the music of a queen. It moves with the rustle of majesty and he came once looking for a queen he found her he will come today how can he not come for her today?

On a brown bench she sits in the parlor, a dark brown wooden bench in a room that is dark with summer light only at the window edge but the heat comes through she sits and waits for him to come and marry her

Camille

The old clock batters evenly at time

Fingers wait on the keys

"This is how I shall not be afraid, this is the way to do it, I will rest my hands on the keys press down for music how sad I am I will sit and play music until he comes for me and I want his brown hands on my body I want him to be here now."

She can play it so far but no further, she can play it as long as each hand has its own tune but then there are notes thrown in belonging nowhere, her thumbs stretch to include them but three songs are too much to hold in two hands and the left hand breaks down altogether it bangs into silence while the upper notes trill alone forgetting one thing after another, excluding the extraneous alto, tripping out the barest height of the song.

Then she cannot play at all but stands and softly walking around the room taps her fingers on the edges of things. Now she is caressing the mantle and tapping the knickknacks, she remembers hot and cold, plays with the itchy sofa cloth touches the underside of the chair rung.

But he was coming with the very best he could find, the very best love that was in him.

"But what about this restlessness—I lean my body against the wall afraid, he will not come, I rub my face against the wall I touch the furniture, I feel the floor beneath my shoes, I want to overturn the bookcases.

"What if a dust storm comes and knocks down the corn?" She stands at the window dreaming. "What if, what if there are places where even cactus can't grow and seeds all burn up?

"What if everything changes so much that I won't understand it anymore? What if life becomes more different than I can understand? Sometimes there is nothing, sometimes there are only passageways between thoughts. Sometimes the music just melts off the page and I sit blank before the blank sheet as two sand dunes would lie beside each other awaiting wind. What if a dust storm were to flatten the corn?"

The music, you see, the music does not go so clearly from one thought to another the music starts with one song for each hand, the two songs played together, it is beautiful and it is only one song and the third song will not be clear the third song is played on the lower fingers of the upper hand and the upper fingers of the lower hand. Sometimes the left hand or the right hand crosses over to find the third song, sometimes it hurts to play, sometimes it is hard to hear the first song or the second song when the third song pulls fingers from left and right and there is no more one song unless it is the third song that pulls the other songs into itself. I want the pain to go away forever, sometimes it's hard. Each moment I must stop and pray.

"O Lord...

"I feel there is not enough sun in the world to keep me from dying this hour, there are no songs in the piano, there is no whisper from the lilac bush unflowering, the lilac bush dark wounded midsummer green, there is nothing only your face how many moments since I saw you smile for me, how could I have ever stopped holding you, how can it be that I ever once took my hands from around your neck or kissed you without kissing you forever?"

So up the stairs again she runs afraid she runs to throw herself on the bed, to hug her suitcases and cry and cry but as she starts to fall on the bed the pillow moves—creeping slowly at the top of her pillow is a black thick heavy roach. It slimes across the colorless hill of the pillowcase, deliberately it creeps up the snowy white cotton inch after inch moving away from the window at the back of the bed. It wants to go behind the pillow where it is dark. It wants to find a dark place and live there.

Camille screams and quickly covering it with the sheet she beats the spot where it should be. She beats and screams and cries out and then beats in silence in the silence she hears Chris coming, she hears and cries out for him and leaving it crushed alive blurred beige by the white nap of the soft cotton sheet, flightless wings and senseless antennae misshapen into a pulsing X unseen as Camille grabs the suitcases and runs down the stairs...

# Matin

ONCE upon a time there was an old half-black Indian mother who set out to walk down from the Allegheny Mountains to the Piedmont Plateau to the Atlantic Coastal Plain to the sea. About halfway through her journey she came upon a solitary house in a desert valley where a soft powdered brown dust had sifted downward from brittle whitish outcrops, and still sifted, parched the air, and choked and clogged the dried waterways of the lower valley. The house was surrounded by many low hills that were faerie hills so that it seemed that the house was sitting in a shallow bowl.

The old mother, whose name was Potomac, came to the door of the house and knocked, for she was very weary of her journey and longed for a place to rest her head for one night. As she stood at the door waiting she heard a voice singing within the house, a maiden's voice, singing as a maiden sings who has been singing alone a very long time and who no longer waits to hear a knock at the door. Potomac turned the knob and opened the door and walked in.

When she walked in she saw the beautiful black maiden dressed all in black, standing in the middle of a floor of sand. On one side of the room there was an old father lying in the sand with his eyes shut fast and he was groaning and writhing as if he were having a nightmare. The old father's feet were bare and rugged and he wore a faded rainbow plaid shirt and faded denim pants and the black maiden tended him gently and sang to him singing, "Sleep unweeping and wake at last to your lovedove or raven." But as she sang it seemed the old father

157

only twisted and cried out the more as he struggled to awake from his terrible dream. And the sand itself was tormented by the writhing of the old father and by the black maiden's song and Potomac saw that the black maiden was filled with sorrow as she struggled in vain to bring peace to the house.

Potomac stood there for a while amazed at the great beauty of the black maiden and at the great suffering of the old father who could not awaken from his nightmare and at the rippling torment of the sand. And in her amazement Potomac spoke to the black maiden saying, "Tell me your story. Tell me how you came to be alone here. Tell me who you are and who is this father and by what power the sand ripples in torment. Let me rest with you one night while you tell me your story, and it may be that as I walk down to the sea I may take away your sorrow."

The black maiden turned to Potomac and spoke saying, "This is my father, who is the union of two brothers who came to America from Europe and Africa. They fought in the Atlantic Ocean, striving and striding westward through the sea to America until their wrestling bodies became one. Thus they came to the Potomac River basin where by a grave mischance this mourner, my father, fell into a nightmare and cannot awaken, and all this beautiful land and the village that surrounds this basin has fallen by enchantment into a desert. For many long years I have watched and waited in these solitary hallways hoping that at last my father would have quiet sleep, and that he may awaken, but my hope has been in vain. I have been left to watch and wait in vain and to know with my waking heart the nightmares that my father dreams."

Saying this the black maiden wept as if her heart would break. But when she had finished weeping she fed Potomac on sweetbread and molasses and rum. And she gave to Potomac a bed of cotton whereon to lay herself and a pillow of cotton for her head, for the old mother Potomac was very tired, as if she had been walking from the mountain to the sea all the days of her life.

And Potomac laid herself down to rest but the black maiden never slept but sat watching all night beside her father. And Potomac slept deep and heavy and long and silently. But the old father writhed in torment and screamed and mourned all that night and the sand that was the many voices of the annihilated village whispered and rustled and fell.

And in the morning when Potomac awoke, the black maiden brought to Potomac a breakfast of sweetbread and molasses and rum and as Potomac ate she saw the great sorrow that shone in the face of the black maiden by reason of her father's dream and she spoke to her saying, "What has your father dreamed this night?" And the black maiden answered saying, "This night he has dreamed of the coming of the ancestors, for those two brothers, my father, those two united ancestors in the sign of my foremothers, forefathers, aunts, cousins—on ships they came, crew and slaves, stifling in the hold, lain cupped into each other— black folk—stink of death, stink of sweat, urination defecation, stink of disease, the black child dead at the black breast. The strong surviving to be slaves—cruelty pride misunderstanding above deck, in sea salt—the white hands, pulling themselves upon the ropes, pulling themselves high upon the mast, high above the deck, did they? did they ever falter as the ropes moved from the trembling underwater black squirming life? Castaways, the white fathers on the mastheads—the black fathers in the holds—the white mothers in their castles—the black mothers in the kitchen, in the back rooms, in the woods, in the bedrooms, in the libraries, in secret cabins, in the captain's quarters, they were had

"And in my father's dream there was one called the nameless one, the black one who was entirely black, who on one of the last slave ships was pulled up from the hold, halfway to America, they brought her up from the deep, carried her up from beneath the waterline and the terror of death to the ocean sparkling light, she saw the dazzling ocean and she saw the blue sky, the sun also on her naked black body as in a tub of cool water they thrust her, ordering her to wash the stink from her flesh that she may be rendered acceptable, so there in a tub of cool water set upon the deck with the crew sneering, gaping, glancing she sponged the bitter death-smell from her body, she had been chained to death, which was how they had found her, how they had recognized her, when they came to throw the dead black boy to the sharks, flinging him over the edge, the dead stink, for the sharks, when they had loosened the child's hand from her hand, then they had noticed her, the black one, the nameless one "If the captain wants a good one" they lifted the dead away from her, "we'll come back to git her" splash, the pretty dead black boy hit the water—chomp, they ate, swallow he was eaten, his skull became another cup vial chalice urn in the lost Atlantic Sea of his people, lost entirely and back they had come for her, halfway across, unloosened her chains, pulling the dead up to breathe air. And after she had subdued the smell of death upon her, to the captain she was given, in the cabin of the captain was she kept, a thin mat on the floor for her, a rough blanket for sorrow. And many times ordered up from the floor into the bunk with the tall sides to keep them from falling, ordered up to lie beneath him and receive him in the ways that he desired, many times ordered down again upon the floor, an interlude of peace lying upon the floor, covered by the blanket. While the stolen life beneath her was rocked almost entirely to death, she lay on the floor of the captain's cabin.

"Then at last in Virginia, my mother's mother's mother's mother's mother's mother, too valuable for Norfolk, too special for Portsmouth, taken with a handful of other black exiles, in a special cart, taken up to Richmond, there to be offered, given in exchange, to those who had especially prepared for them, who had especially ordered black chiefs, black cherubs, black ladies of the chamber. Four cartloads of these special ones rattled up to Richmond, and she among them, taken then, sold and bartered, declared acceptable, taken after inspection

159

and approval by a certain lawyer, soon after delivered to the home of this same lawyer, sitting alone in the back of the cart driven by another slave received, greeted, taken to her place. Not for long did she tend the small family garden before the young lawyer availing himself of his property rights tendered her with himself, she thence conceiving and bringing forth a female child, Laetitia, brown-eyed Laetitia of alabaster skin. Also at that time had the young master taken unto himself a wife, a southern belle of a wife, white blue-eyed blond, and yea also, she thus conceiving, and she did bring forth a male child. Time passed and husband and wife and slave concubine and female slave child and male child grew older and the fate of the black one, the nameless one, is hidden from us. But the child Laetitia grew in beauty and tenderness and desire and before her twentieth year had she received within herself the sperm of both her white father and of the white male child, her father's son, her half-brother. The child life of both had she held within herself.

"Then did there come to be great contention within the family of the masters, which a long time passing had been a family of lawyers, all the masters having been lawyers since the time of Elizabeth the First, until the time came when the young master having completed those studies necessary to become also a lawyer in the tradition of his fathers, then did he think it well to take for himself also a wife, who was a southern belle of a wife, white blue-eyed blond, and he willed to create a home of his own, moving from beneath the roof of his fathers to another place, which was to be his place and the place of his wife. Yet did he beg from his father one boon saying, 'Give to me Laetitia to be my slave within my house, Laetitia, the lovely.' Yet did his father say no unto him, not willing to release the lovely enslaved body to his son. Long and bitterly did they argue concerning the ownership of that body, finally contenting themselves to share her, that she would stay with the young master autumn and winter but when spring and summer should come upon them then she would go to the house of the old master. In this way they hoped to content themselves without bitterness, yet this could not be so for the wife of the young master could take no joy in life for she knew that the lovely one, Laetitia, the brown-eyed dark-haired white-skinned slave had preceded her, had stolen the love of her husband before he had ever thought to become a husband. Then did she rage day and night not to have Laetitia within her house, but the young master, the young lawyer, would not return the slave to his father, in bitter jealousy would he not release Laetitia. Then did the old master and the young master decide between them, to take Laetitia and give her a home of her own, to place her as if she were entirely white, giving her a place of her own, a false story to tell, making her a widow returned from the western lands, teaching her all proper language, diction, speech, and the long tale of the wandering god who begot Jesus Christ upon Mary his daughter—the masters giving Laetitia of their own library, books to read that she might well portray what she was not. Heavy with child was she

160

then, and no one knew which was the father, the old master or the young master, and fear they had lest the skin of the child be black and joy had the wives of the masters for hope that the child's skin would be black and the plan to make for Laetitia her own home thus would fail. So before placing her in the home they had prepared they awaited the birth of the child, and the child was born, and it was a female child and her skin was white and her hair was sandy silky and her eyes were blue and they named her Rowena.

Then did Laetitia and Rowena move to the house that was prepared for them, and Rowena grew thinking that her mother was a white widow, and she the child of a deceased soldier. Often was Laetitia visited by the old master. Often by the young master. In private talk and in whispering. But the child Rowena understood nothing, growing in all virtue and innocence and purity. And when the hand of the young master would have lifted to touch the young Rowena, the innocent child, then did Laetitia cry nay, never. And because of their jealousies having money and power of her own, having status and capital, did she say 'Forever will I receive upon my body the father and the son my masters nor will I say I have no pleasure in them for I have pleasure to give myself to father and brother, infolding the life of the one with the other until I know well how deeply we have sinned, but not shall you lift your hand to touch my child, which is the child of US.' Thus it came to be as time and age reconciled the father with the son did they come to the house of Laetitia together and together did they fondle her body. In passion did the three of them play together and it was joy for the three of them in their sin.

Yet still was Rowena a virgin, reading her Bible, sitting in her gardens, attending a private finishing school for young southern ladies, somewhere in Western Virginia, where no one knew who she was. But once did she unexpectedly come home and find them, the three, together. The two masters standing with their private parts exposed, holding the naked Laetitia horizontal between them. The young master between her legs with his hands gripped around her thighs, the old master at her head, his hands hooked under her shoulders and Laetitia was held in the air in the shape of an X in order to be fornicated.

Then did the cries of the young virgin who watched them merely drive them further into passion. And pumping themselves into her mother, the masters cried out to Rowena in their love heat, "Yeah, now you know, you and your Ma both are niggers, we can fuck her like this 'cause she's our nigger, and you're our nigger too, you're a nigger slave, your grandma's a nigger African, we got papers to show that you and your Ma are niggers. You think you're white but you're a goddam nigger, you ain't white, you're black, you're our black nigger bitch. We can sell you or rape you any day of the week. We can let you know why God created black nigger bitches." Speaking thus to the frantic white virgin, they expended themselves in her mother. And just before the last, before they released Laetitia onto the floor the young master shouted at Rowena who stood screaming, crying, her hand frozen on the wood beside the glass of the secretary, 'Git out before you git more to worry 'bout than your Ma. Your turn is coming soon enough. Git to your room and lock the door or you'll find more trouble than you want, go on, get out.'

"After the masters had gone was there not much weeping? did they not weep and mourn? mother and child, sorrowing over the sins of property rights, power, and passion that had brought them both into life. And Rowena in her mercy and goodness found it in her heart to forgive her mother, and did not curse her for the crimes slavery had wrought in her. Yet did Rowena say, 'I will no longer live this lie, give me then if you will, of your substance, that I may begin a life that is true, and I will leave here going to another place where I may live.' Then was Rowena dressed in silks and satins and of substance was she given money and books and clothes. Her mother then took her to a train station where they parted the final parting, Rowena went north coming to rest at last in the mountains that are the mountains of Pennsylvania. There she gave herself in marriage to a black Indian husband, and at an advanced child-bearing age she gave birth to a female child, my great-grandmother. Twenty years after the Civil War. My great-grandmother then grew, married, and gave birth to Camille, my grandmother. And Camille my grandmother married John Christopher Snowdon, who is my grandfatherfather, and three daughters were born to John Christopher and Camille including Patricia, my mother. And if any male child were born to Laetitia, or if any male child were born to Rowena, or if any male child were born to my great-grandmother, or if any male child were born to my grandmother Camille, the word has not yet come to me. And this because the masters with white skin caused there to be no males kept for the defense of the house.

"And from these origins has there come this great curse upon our house: 'The females shall be raped and the males shall be murdered.' And the males that are not murdered shall be sold, and to certain ones of the males that are neither murdered nor sold, to certain of those few males come late into the house marrying, and to certain of the males born to the house but who nevertheless survive murder and slavery—to these shall be given the power of revenge upon the females of their own house who consented with the white males for their destruction, these males shall be given the female children of their own house, and these shall be raped. And raped again.

"And Laetitia died a long time ago. Laetitia died but before she died she wrote to her child Rowena saying, 'Come to me, come, I die, I have no one with me.' And Rowena wrote back saying, 'Come but how shall I come when the child at my breast is black and I cannot leave here and if I come with this child your friends shall know that you are black.' And Laetitia wrote saying, 'Come, come to me, I die, but leave the child with someone, come to me before I die.' And Rowena wrote back saying, 'Can you still not accept our blackness even though you die? What difference shall it make after all? I cannot leave the child, I

162

cannot come.' And Laetitia wrote a third time saying, 'If they discover that I am black they will not bury me where I have longed to be buried and I will have no peace in the grave. Come to me, come ere I die, but bring not the child.' And Rowena wrote back writing the third time, 'I shall not come.' This is the dream of my father."

And Potomac spoke to the black maiden saying, "Give to me a handful of the tormented sand of your village that I may carry it with me in my journey down to the sea and when I come to the sea I will cast it away and then your father's dream will be ended and your village will return and call back her people and our land will remember her first beauty."

So the black maiden gave a handful of the tormented sand of her village into the hands of Potomac that Potomac might cast it into the sea. And maybe Potomac cast it into the sea, or maybe she carried it away to another land, or maybe she hid it again on the Atlantic Coastal Plain. But as for the black maiden, after she gave the sand of the village into the keeping of Potomac she waited a night or a hundred nights until the sun dawned cold and clear and bright on the first morning of the millennium. And on that morning, a long, long time ago, as she saw the dawn brighten her solitary house in the desert, the tormented ancestor, her father, was calmed out of nightmare into sleep. And the tormented sand became a sleepy shadowy village and surrounded all that place, a village sleeping as if more than anything else in the world it had most desired to rest from dreaming, as if all its streets and towers and fields were an epic song told by a perpetual flame within an empty polished enjeweled marble skull washed up and cast down by the waters of the Atlantic Sea.

And I, Diotima, learned this tale from Diotima, the one who long ago came to us from the north where she knew the black maiden, who is Johnnie, Diotima came here to Puerto Escondido telling this tale and creating the storytelling tribe of Diotima so that we may know what has passed in the north and why there is such great silence there, her precious Johnnie did not come to us, but waited and watched, a black child with white eyes, chiaroscuro, watched in the village of Washington until she became a pure and perfect light, Johnnie, looking toward a bright reckoning day of singing and rejoicing for her village and her people, watching the streets and paths and lanes of the village, watching beside the houses and huts, whispering into each window awakening the children—did she whisper these words? Is it true? Did it happen?

Few are the stories that are left to us from that village and that nation, but the first Diotima has passed down to us the tale of how greatly Johnnie believed she would awaken her people at the last singing to them the song of awakening thus, at the end of that distant century.

I will not keep you sorrowing with the sorrow of our story but rather I now recall you to the joy that has been promised you—it has been promised and already it comes and when you have received it you will remember that I knew and that I told you and that it was hard for you to believe. It is hard for you to believe but it is already conceived among you and I tell you surely in full words what it is so that you will believe me that I understood from the beginning, and that it is ordained, and that I know and do not lie when I say to you joy shall come to our land.

It shall be the joy of beautifully wrought things, words that capture each thing you have loved forever, your stern condemning gods will understand and smile and forgive and you will be utterly happy in that moment, which will last longer than all the ancient marauding powers of our land. This land. Will you awaken again into this land? I hope you listen to all I speak for you, there are many secrets for you hidden in what I say. But whether you hear or not I must give you my happiest wishes. I have given up longing for the comfort of death and the rest and peace of lying within the earth and I have taken on the grief of immortality for your sake. I have watched for you and waited for you so long because I love you very much and I wish you a Happy New Millennium, may you see the consummation of your dream—Happy New Millennium, Happy New Millennium, Happy New Millennium!

But it came not to pass, for the byword not only for that all that house but for all that village, that capital city of the north, Washington City kept as its byword forever for its grand family of Northern Europe and Africa, forever, "Kill the boys and rape the girls," and therefore even their own gods, who had long since repented of their sins in begetting fruit with their daughters, their own gods turned away their heads and misapplied the great prayer of the black maiden, and perverted her belief, such that the dream, indeed, that terrifying northern dream, found consummation, yes, the dream was consumed mysteriously and eliminated by strange fire, as well as all of the dreamers, consumed, not one was left, saving only Johnnie, condemned to immortality, Johnnie, thereafter forever, because as I have told you of this last image of the city, now she is a light

a light

alight

Washington City, New York City, Santa Fe, Albuquerque, London, Lowestoft, Paris, Köln, Stockholm, Narvik, Roma, Firenze, Zurich, Almansil, Philadelphia, Cambridge and Brookline, Massachusetts, Washington City, 1972-1990, December 2000.

# ABOUT THE AUTHOR

Carolivia Herron has had a passionate attachment to the epic literary genre ever since her reading of Milton's **Paradise Lost** when she was eleven years old helped her to cope with the death of her infant brother. All of Herron's tasks in writing, scholarship and educational multimedia development relate to her love of epic, and are in conversation with the epics of Africa, Europe, Asia and the Americas. Her doctorate in Comparative Literature from the University of Pennsylvania focuses on comparative epic, and she has shared this love of epic in professorial appointments at the University of Binghamton, California State University, Chico, Mount Holyoke College, and Harvard University where she founded the Epicenter for the study of Epic and Oral Poetry. During Spring 2001 she will be teaching "Star Trek as American Epic" at Grinnell College. The original Epicenter has evolved into Herron's private company, Epicenter Literary Software, which develops multimedia education programs based on scenes and stories of Washington, DC. Her particular focus is African American Epic Tradition, and her controversial children's book, *Nappy Hair*, is actually an application of her developing concept of African American call and response as an epic structure. *Nappy Hair* is excerpted from Herron's novel in progress, *Asenath and Our Song of Songs* which is a fictional retelling of the path of African epic into African American consciousness as well as a dramatization of the intersection between African and Jewish cultures. Herron currently lives in her home town of Washington, DC where she directs the e-mail mentoring program for children, PAUSE (Potomac Anacostia Ultimate Story Exchange).


Find out more about Carolivia Herron and her work at the following web addresses:

http://www.carolivia.org
http://www.carolivia.org/nappyhair
http://www.epiclitsoft.com
http://www.drumofanansi.org